Foundresses, Founders, and their Religious Families

FOUNDRESSES, FOUNDERS, AND THEIR RELIGIOUS FAMILIES

JOHN M. LOZANO, C.M.F.

Translated by
JOSEPH DARIES, C.M.F.

Claret Center for Resources in Spirituality

RELIGIOUS LIFE SERIES

Volume Five

Chicago   Los Angeles   Manila

1983

This is a translation by Joseph Daries, C.M.F.
of *El Fundador y su Familia Religiosa,* Instituto
Teologico de la Vida Religiosa: Madrid, 1978, and of
the additions introduced by the author.

Contents

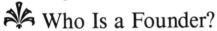

Chapter III

 The Grace of Spiritual Fruitfulness

Chapter IV

 The Founding Charism

Chapter V

 The Original Inspiration

Chapter VI

✦ Doctrine

Chapter VII

 # Fullness of Spirit

Chapter VIII

 # Charism and Institution

Chapter IX

 # The Sufferings of Founders and Foundresses

Chapter X

From Founder to Group: The Community Charism

Chapter XI

 Communitary Charism and the Personalities of the Founders and Foundresses

Chapter XII

 The Interpretation of the Charism

Chapter XIII

 Charism and Tradition: Living Realities

Foreword

Since the publication of Pius XI's Letter, *Unigenitus,*[1] recent popes have dealt repeatedly with the role which founders and foundresses of religious Institutes have played in the Church, and especially in their own religious families. But it was really certain texts of Vatican II relating to the nature of the Church in a broader context[2] that aroused the interest of religious in their founders and in the mission that properly characterized each of them. This is true above all in modern Congregations, which have been so busy in the service of God and the Church that many of them have not had time to dwell on the work of conceptualizing their own vocation and spirit, let alone on a study of their founder. However, even in the most ancient Institutes, which often have a rich bibliography on this theme, new problems have arisen on the level of theory, such as the meaning of the term "charism" as applied to an entire religious family, on their relationship with the grace they have received through their founder, as well as on the transmission and extension of that grace.

Not many years ago the bibliography relating to these themes was rather limited. Happily, it has been growing in recent years. There is a small book relating to founders' charisms,[3] a short article in the *Enciclopedia Cattolica,*[4] a longer and more complete article in the *Dizionario degli Instituti di Perfezione,*[5] a series of studies and articles in various reviews.[6] Recently, while our study was being translated, a doctoral dissertation was published on the subject in Italian.[7] Something more can be learned here and there from monographs dedicated to individual founders. To this published material we should add something of the contents of the three successive *Inquiries* of the Roman Curia concerning the delicate and debated question of whether St. Louis Grignon de Montfort may be truly considered the founder of the Brothers of St. Gabriel. In this case we are less interested in the specific question of the relationship between the Saint and his Institute than we are in the doctrinal presuppositions expressed in certain documents of the dossier of the *Inquiries*. Although these responses are the votes of consultors and as such express only the opinions of their authors, we must bear in mind that they are opinions sought by the Holy See and are given by persons of some prominence.[8]

In the present study we take advantage of all this material, integrating it with our own personal investigations, and finally, we bring it all to bear on the question of the mission of founders and their relationships with their religious families.

I

Who Is a Founder?

1. Founders in History

Since the time of St. Pachomius in the fourth century, the presence and action of men and women founders of religious Institutes is a characteristic phenomenon repeated over and over in the history of the Church until our own day. But who can properly be called a founder? In response to a consultational inquiry of the Sacred Congregation of Rites dated November 2, 1946, Claretian Father Siervo Goyeneche wrote that, while canonical documentation on the founding of churches and benefices was rich and precise, "I have been unable, either in the Code or in earlier sources, to discover the essential notes defining the founder of a religious Institute."[1] Perhaps for this very reason another consultor interrogated at the time, Father Gerald Oesterle, O.S.B., a man more sensitive to historical research, had recourse to history in order to spell out some of the different ways in which a Christian could be said to be the founder of an Institute.[2] Although no doubt a good deal could be found in magisterial statements, especially the more recent ones, apropos of our subject (indeed, we will be dealing with some of them), it seems evident that the best method is first to have recourse to a historical survey in order to introduce and pursue the whole question of founders.

If we examine the historical record closely the first thing we discover is that there are many different ways of being a founder. The great St. Anthony was not properly speaking a founder, since he was neither the first anchorite nor did he leave any particular institution behind him. And yet the fact is that, thanks to his personal holiness and his enormous influence on primitive monasticism, we are obliged to include him in some manner in this category. Some of the first founders were such, owing far more to the fact that they wrote Rules by which one or several institutions came to live throughout the centuries, rather than to their having actually gathered together a group or to their having personally established communities to which they gave their Rule. For various reasons and titles, St. Basil, St. Augustine, and St. Benedict belong to this class of founders. Others were founders because they created a centralized institution of which they were superiors and masters. In the fourth century, far ahead of his time, St. Pachomius was a founder in just this way—a way that would reappear with St. Norbert in the twelfth century and, almost immediately afterwards, with the founders of the Mendicant Orders and of the Apostolic Societies.

We should note, however, that the generalized concept of a founder as one who founds a centralized and organized institution did not completely do away with the other concept. St. Philip Neri is clearly the founder of the Oratory, since he conceived the basic idea of the Oratory, drafted the outlines of its spirit, and gave the norms for its evangelical community, although the various local Oratories kept their autonomy. Something of this sort seems to be happening today in the case of Giovanni Rossi and his work, *Pro Civitate Christiana*.

The three consultors whose opinion was sought by the Congregation of Rites for the New Inquiry of 1947, relating to the matter we referred to above, agree in somewhat different terms that there are two requisites for someone to be considered a founder: 1) He or she must have conceived the idea and ends of the Institute, and 2) he or she must have given the group its norms of life and government. That is to say, a founder must be both (as Father Goyeneche put it, drawing on Pius XI's *Unigenitus*) "Pater et Legifer," father and lawgiver, and we would add, father *or mother* and lawgiver.[3]

Let us sum up the data that appear most frequently in relationships between founders and their sons or daughters, so as to ascertain which are always present and may thus be considered essential, and which on the contrary occur only in certain cases and hence, strictly speaking, cannot be essential.

1. In the first place, all founders in some way feel called by God to create a new religious family, or more generally speaking, a new family of evangelical life.

2. Founders assign the goals of this family and draw up its rule of life, at least along its fundamental lines.

3. All founders give their communities certain Rules or Constitutions. This does not mean that they themselves exclusively compose these Rules or Constitutions. Frequently the founder seeks the collaboration of some of his or her spiritual sons or daughters. The first group of St. Ignatius Loyola's followers collaborated with him in drawing up some fundamental guidelines, and some of them later gathered pertinent texts from earlier traditions.[4] St. Anthony Mary Claret asked two of his co-founders, the Servant of God Father Jaime Clotet and Father Joseph Xifre, superior general of his Missionaries, to collaborate with him in this task.[5] In a great many cases a woman founder has sought the help of a priest, who was better prepared for this sort of work, to draw up a more complete set of Constitutions. But in this case the priest always followed the idea of the founder.

There are cases where founders have given their sons or daughters the Rule or Constitions of some older Institute. In many of these instances, we find the Rule of Benedict, Augustine, or Francis followed by particular Constitutions. In much fewer cases we find founders giving their followers the Constitutions of another modern Institute. For example, St. Julie Fostel gave her Sisters of Mercy of the Christian Schools the Constitutions of St. Jean-Baptiste de la Salle. We should note here, too, that all Congregations approved during opening decades of the twentieth century received identical Constitutions from the Holy See, except for the paragraph that defined their specific end, mentioned their title, and listed their co-patrons.[6]

In this third group we have mentioned a number of diverse cases which need to be further distinguished. There are, for example, cases in which an Institute, at a distance of some centuries, adopts as its own the Rule proper of an ancient founder, with the intention of realizing its vision of the religious life without further ado; although, naturally, there will be further disciplinary Constitutions adapted to the times. This is what the Augustinians have done and, in this case, St. Augustine is their father, founder, and master.

There are other groups in which the Rule is held up as a general source of inspiration for the Constitutions, in which we find the creation of the new religious family with its own specific ends. In this case the real founder is that of the new family, and his or her legislative work consists: a) in referring to the patriarch who gave the Rule, for the overall basic vision of the new group, and b) in providing the new Constitutions professed in the Congregation.

There are cases in which a founder gives his or her group Constitutions written by another saint. This suffices to make the former a founder, provided he or she also feels called by God to found a family with particular characteristics.

There is not the slightest problem in the fact that many founders, in writing their Rules or Constitutions, have taken their inspiration from documents of earlier religious traditions.

4. Many founders were at the same time members of the Congregation which they founded. Others were not, and this is at least true of all men who founded Institutes for women. There is also at least one case of a woman who founded an Institute for men.

5. Most founders directly governed their communities, but even some of these decided to hand over the ordinary government to others for one reason or another, as for example when they were elected bishops. Nevertheless, even in this case they usually continued to intervene in the constitutive process of the Institute. St. Anthony Mary Claret is a typical case in point. A scant year and a half after founding his Congregation, he had to leave his first followers in Spain to go to his new position in Cuba as Archbishop of Santiago. Initially he resisted the appointment, giving as his reason the fact that he had just founded the primitive group. But from the moment he accepted the assignment, another member became the superior of the Congregation. Nevertheless, both before his voyage to Cuba and after his return to Spain, he presided over the constitutive chapters and assemblies held in his lifetime, wrote the Constitutions, and, in 1870, gave his consent for the conversion of the Apostolic Institute into a Congregation of simple vows, thus setting his seal of approval on a movement that had been developing within the Congregation.

2. Traits that Characterize a Founder.

After this rapid but sufficient review of the history of the religious life (which has not, however, overlooked any signficant case), we may conclude:

In the first place, there are many manners and means of being the founder of a religious Institute. There are various degrees in which a founder may be involved in the life of the Institute created by him or her.

Among the various traits that distinguish founders, their essential role seems to consist of: a) having felt called by God to create a new religious family, and b) having defined their ends and lifestyle, and shaped their spirit. These are the only traits present in all founders.

Thus we are in essential agreement with the conclusions reached by the three consultors interrogated by the Congregation of Rites in 1946, to whom we referred above.

Nevertheless, we could not leave this theme without making some further, more precise observations on what we have just said.

A. On Conceiving the Idea of the Institute

The first observation would be that it is not necessary that the founder be the first to have the idea for the new community. Some have theoretically considered the suitableness of founding a type of Institute which some other Servant of God had founded shortly afterwards or at the same time. Even in this case the circumstances differ. In a letter to St. Ignatius, Master Gaspar Lopez writes that St. John of Avila, the Apostle of Andalusia, had wanted to form the "Holy Company" some years earlier but did not have the opportunity,[7] and even Ignatius admitted the great similarity of "wills and modes of procedure" in what both they and their followers were doing.[8] In this case there was certainly no influence of Avila on Loyola, but simply a coincidence of inclinations that was not discovered until later, after the society was founded. But St. Ignatius adds the fact that he had felt called effectively to found the Society of Jesus, and it is clear that in founding an Institute similar to the one that St. John of Avila had wanted to found he gave it characteristics all its own.

The case of St. Alphonsus Liguori is exemplary in this respect. On the one hand, he was a member of an association of missionary priests who engaged in evangelizing and had begun to receive divine lights and impulses that were gradually orienting him toward the foundation of an Institute devoted to this ministry. On the other hand, a nun, Sister Maria Celeste, had a vision in which she understood that God was calling Alphonsus to found a Congregation of this type. Finally, Sister Maria's confessor, Falcoia, spoke to St. Alphonsus concerning this project, asking him to be the cornerstone of the Institute.[9] The calling, then, was for Alphonsus.

Something similar took place in the case of St. Anthony Mary Claret and his Missionaries. In the first place, there is documentary evidence that even before 1842 Canon Jose Caixal, while exiled in France, had gathered together a group of priests devoted to parish missions.[10] Without Caixal's knowledge, this is what Claret was doing in the autumn of that year. Later both of them met and Caixal became a collaborator of Claret, and Claret's missionary team became a Congregation. Later still, in 1848, when Claret was missioning in the Canary Islands, Caixal wrote him of the spiritual lights received by Mother Antonia Paris, according to whom God was calling Claret to found a Congregation of Missionaries. St. Anthony immediately replied that he had already had this very idea and that some houses had already been offered him for the purpose, but that he would have to wait a little. In this case, the charism of prophecy, received by the Venerable Mother Antonia, served to confirm St. Anthony in his vocation as founder.[11]

It has sometimes happened that the idea of founding an Institute, even though it was first conceived by the one who would have to carry it out, was actually born in his or her mind under the influence of another person who helped the founder or foundress to become aware of a need in the Church. For example, a pastoral letter by Bishop Hussey of Waterford, uncovering a plot to uproot the Catholic faith of his people by opening up official schools, led Edmund Rice to found his Institute of Christian Brothers.[12]

But it may also happen that someone also conceives the idea for the Institute and transmits it to the one who will later be its founder. Thus, Antonio Rosmini founded his Institute of Charity at the suggestion of Blessed Magdalen of Canossa.[13] The important thing to note in such cases is that those who suggest the foundation in question (perhaps their bishop or their spiritual director), do not think of it as a mission entrusted to themselves, but rather to someone else who will actually become the founder. In this case the former serve as instruments of God in order to manifest his will to another. The founder is the one who discovers that it is God's will that he or she should found this new religious family.

Precisely because this consciousness of being called by God to create an Institute is an essential note of a founder, we cannot consider a saint to be a founder of a community when, after the Institute is actually founded, it turns to him or her for protection or as a source of doctrine. The Oblates of St. Francis de Sales, founded around 1871 by Father Louis Brisson, state in their Constitutions that they place themselves under the patronage of the holy bishop of Geneva and take his doctrine as the source of their spirit. In some cases, when an Institute accepts the spirituality of an earlier saint, it can say that it takes him or her as father or mother, this is not to be understood in the strict sense of founder, but in a broader sense of being the source of the spiritual doctrine embraced by the institution.

B. On Defining the Aims and Lifestyle of the Institute

We must also further qualify the second distinguishing trait of founders, namely, that of having defined the aims and rule of life for their religious family. This must be understood as an actual given, and in the broad sense. For there are cases in which monasticism was not interpreted as a vocation parallel to the common vocation of a Christian, but as an advanced and exemplary form of the common Christian calling.

Thus, St. Basil proposed to his brothers nothing more than "the faithful observance of the Gospel,"[14] and St. Benedict assigned to his Rule no other aim but that of establishing a "school for the service of God."[15] But it is equally certain that St. Basil was *de facto* proposing a way of Christian life characterized by celibacy and fraternal community. The "service of God, or divine service" in St. Benedict's day meant in reality the monastic life, which is a particular vocation. What we today would describe as characteristics of the religious life, they described as means for developing the common Christian vocation (which they certainly are, as we could as well say of matrimony), but since they in fact characterize a special lifestyle, they become the aims for an institution promoting that type of existence. We must also bear this in mind when we read, in the Rule of the Friars Minor, that it is "their Rule and life, to keep the Holy Gospel of our Lord Jesus Christ, living in obedience, without property, and in chastity.[16]

Starting with the twelfth century the religious life began to be differentiated, and within it there grew a tendency to distinguish the specific ends proper of each Institute. Mercedarians, Dominicans, etc., now propose a particular end for each Order. Given the importance of this end for the configuration of each new religious family, the end must have been assigned by the founder. We should note, however, that "proper or specific" end, does *not* mean "exclusive" end. It suffices that the end be proper to the Institute, although it may also be proper to others.

As for the rule of life, it is not necessary that the founder alone define all its elements. In the celebrated Deliberations of 1539, concerning the founding of the Society of Jesus, the companions of St. Ignatius intervened and voted.[17] Nor is it required that the founder define the details of the rule of life (although this could happen later, little by little), but only its fundamental traits. Nor is it necessary, as we have seen, that the founder write the Constitutions. But it does seem necessary that he or she, either in written or oral form, should outline the fundamental traits of the kind of life to be led, traits which someone else may later copy into the Constitutions.

C. Must the Founder Actually Start the Institute?

This is a delicate question, yet it is one which seems to have been already resolved in practice by the Holy See.

In the first place, although the founder is ordinarily the first to organize the group from which the new religious family is to be born, this does not seem to be an indispensable condition. We have at least one case in which it was not so, namely that of St. Soledad Torres Acosta and the Servants of Mary. The Saint was the last of seven young women chosen by a priest to start a Congregation. Five years later the priest left for Africa, taking some of the first sisters with him. St. Soledad remained as a guide to the group in Madrid. Bit by bit the community began forming around her and absorbing her spirit and government.[18] Not only the Servants of Mary, but the Holy See as well, acknowledge her as their founder.

We might ask ourselves, secondly, if the founder must have a direct action on the Institute, that is to say, if the founder must be the one who gathers the group together, to realize the ends that are being proposed to it. One of the consultors submitting his opinion for the Inquiry of 1942, as to whether St. Louis Grignion de Montfort was the founder of the Brothers of St. Gabriel, responded in the negative. He based his answer on the fact that "the title and meaning of founder implies his direct and immediate action on the Institute.[19] In the case in question there was indeed no such direct and immediate action, since the Brothers were not founded until years later. We would not like to enter this delicate historical question, already studied by order of the See, but we can and should add our disagreement with the opinion stated. For there is at least one case in which the Holy See has recognized as a founder one Saint who thought out an evangelical institution, although he himself was not able to carry it out—indeed, it was not started until almost a century later. We refer to St. Anthony Mary Claret and the Secular Institute, Cordimarian Filiation.

What is really important is that the founder defines the ends and shapes the life and spirituality of the Institute, even though this Institute may in some cases not be able to be brought into existence at that time. Note that something rather similar happened in the case of St. Augustine and the Augustinians. In this case, the Saint did gather together various groups, first of laypersons, then of priests, and gave them his Rule. But the Augustinian Order, properly so called, did not come into existence until centuries later, when a new group, under quite different circumstances, adopted as their own the experience, the Rule, and the spirit of the great Doctor of the Church.

Finally, we may consider the case of the Little Brothers and Little Sisters of Jesus, established respectively by Father Rene Voillaume in 1933 and by Sister Magdalen of Jesus in 1939. Father Voillaume constantly refers to Charles de Foucauld as their father. We do not intend to define the relationship that exists between these two Institutes and Father Voillaume and Sister Magdalen, on the one hand,

and between them and Charles de Foucauld, on the other. A recent article states that both were founded "under the aegis of the spirituality of de Foucauld," that is to say, following his spirituality.[20]

3. Founders, Patriarchs, Matriarchs

In our rapid review of history we encountered one fact to which we should redirect our attention. There are groups of modern Congregations related in some way to the Mendicant Orders: the numerous Congregations of Mercedarian, Dominican, Franciscan, and, in lesser numbers, Servite Sisters. These are communities founded with specific ends, frequently quite different from those that gave rise to the respective Orders. Their relationship with the Order is either that the founder was a member of the Order, or that the woman who founded the Congregation had as her spiritual director a man who belonged to the Order.

All of these modern Congregations have their own founder, distinct from the one who founded the Order. Several of these modern founders have been canonized, which means that there was a new and notably intense experience of the Spirit at the very origin of these Congregations. In all these cases the Church's statements on founders applies to the man or woman who founds the Congregation and refers to the founder of the Order only to the extent that the new group has appropriated the latter's spirit. The reference to the founder of the Congregation is the *immediate* and decisive factor. Conversely, the reference to the Franciscan, Dominican, Carmelite, or whatever other spirit, is *mediate,* that is, only to the extent that this spirit is part of the distinctive charism of the immediate founder of the Congregation. Many of these Congregations consider the founder of the Order, whose name they bear, as the *patriarch* or the *matriarch* of the whole Franciscan, Dominican, Carmelite, etc., family. This, in fact, seems to be the title that properly belongs to them.

4. The Founding Couple

The history of women's foundations reflects the evolution of the social position of women throughout the course of history. Initially, monasteries for women had to have a man as their founder. St. Caesarius of Arles and St. Leander of Seville composed a Rule for nuns. In other cases the women adopted a Rule written by men, for men and then made the necessary natural adaptations. This seems to have been the case with the Augustinian nuns, if one accepts the opinion that the Holy Doctor wrote the *Praeceptum* for men, while the *Charta* is simply a translation into feminine terms of the *Praeceptum*.[21] This certainly was the case with the Benedictine nuns, and seems to have been so with the Pachomian nuns in the fourth century. St. Francis of Assisi himself wrote a very short "Form of Life" and "Testament" for the Poor Clares.[22]

More than once, especially in the context of the current worldwide movement for women's liberation which is now rightly affecting religious communities of women, women have approached the author and registered an understandable grievance at the fact that women should have been following a rule of life written by men for men. Wouldn't these rules reflect a typically male mentality? Something of the sort has frequently arisen in history. Certain Constitutions would doubtless have been different if feminine minds and hearts had figured in their composition. But we should also note that it would be unjust and harmful to apply these animadversions *tout court* to the great Rules that were mentioned above. There is such an evangelical and ecclesial intensity in the Augustinian *Praeceptum* and the Rule of St. Benedict, for example, that they seem to transcend sexual differences. Besides, it is clear that the monk/abbot relationship was lived in an intensely feminine manner in the nun/abbess relationship. The nuns themselves translated this relationship in the way they lived it.

A second point to be made in this connection is the fact that, alongside the founder who wrote the Rule, we frequently find a woman of eminent sanctity and strong personality. In the case of Pachomius, Benedict, Caesarius, and Leander, this "strong woman" was their own natural sister, who really started the feminine branch of the Order. In the case of St. Francis, this strong charismatic figure was St. Clare. In good part it was these women who incarnated the ideals of the father founder in their own proper mode, i.e., the feminine mode.

We would have to wait until the times of the Council of Trent in order to find a woman independently creating her own religious family (St. Angela Merici and the Company of St. Ursula), or even guiding a group of men as well as her own group of women (St. Teresa of Avila). In this same category of women who acted on their own, although they availed themselves of the counsel and direction of a male director, we would have to include St. Maria Micaela of the Blessed Sacrament and St. Rafaela Maria of the Sacred Heart.

From the seventeenth century on there appears a new version of the founding couple which we have already seen in the monastic Orders and in the Poor Clares: St. Francis de Sales and St. Jane de Chantal; St. Vincent de Paul and St. Louise de Marillac; St. Anthony Claret and the Servant of God, Antonia Paris; St. John Bosco and St. Maria Mazzarello. . . . The list could be continued at great length.

The fact is that most of the Congregations of women that appeared between the seventeenth and nineteenth centuries have a founding couple at their origins. This repeated phenomenon is explained by one or more of the following basic reasons:

1) In some cases a holy woman has felt so completely in sympathy with the spiritual aims and personality of a holy man that a communion of spirits was established between them. In some of these cases a special revelation was involved. Mother Antonia Paris felt called by God to found a Congregation of women, but at the same time, through mystical enlightenments she received in prayer, she understood that St. Anthony Mary Claret, whom she had not yet met (although she had heard of his fame as a missionary), was to found the Congregation with her.

2) In other cases the idea for the foundation emerged out of the relationships between a woman and her confessor or spiritual director, so that it is often hard to say who had the idea first. The mission and spirit of the new religious family grew simutaneously in both of them. In this case, as in the immediately preceding one, both persons, the woman and the man, are the founders.

3) In still other cases a man who is dedicated to pastoral action, e.g., a bishop or a priest, had the idea of founding an Institute with a specific ministry for which he felt there was a need. Since this ministry was a feminine ministry, he naturally had to gather a group of women to perform the ministry.

4) Finally, in numerous other cases it was a woman who felt called to create this new family, but, given the social position of women, she

would not have realized her ideal without availing herself of the support of some man, usually the bishop of the diocese or the spiritual director of the mother founder. In this case, as in the immediately preceding one, only one party is, properly speaking, the founder, whereas the other is really a co-founder.

There are many Congregations that have not established a position on the respective role played by each of their "founders," and the Holy See has not yet resolved the question. The matter can only be resolved by the Congregation as a whole, acting through its general chapter, after a serious historical investigation. Criteria for this work seem to be the ones that have emerged during the foregoing analysis: 1) How did the idea for the Institute first emerge? 2) To what extent did each of the parties involved influence the shaping of the Institute's mission and spirit?

II

Founders and Foundresses in the Documents of the Magisterium

The popes have frequently spoken of the mission of founders, both in addresses to the members of particular Institutes and to the People of God in general. This practice dates from the Middle Ages, at least in pronouncements on the holiness of this or that founder. Popes have referred to this subject in bulls or apostolic letters addressed to individual monasteries or to entire religious families. In modern times, founders are quite frequently referred to in allocutions and discourses addressed to representatives of their respective Institutes. This became a common practice with Pius XII and Paul VI.

Even when these papal allocutions and documents refer to a particular founder, without the intention of formulating a doctrine encompassing all founders, it is obvious that many of their statements reflect an overall idea concerning the mission of founders in the Church and in their religious families.

The Church's Magisterium has dealt with the subject of founders in general, in increasingly precise terms, since the end of the eighteenth century. Various popes, as well as the Second Vatican Council, have continued this practice. Popes worthy of special notice in this respect have been Pius VI, Pius IX, Pius XI, and Paul VI.

During the First Vatican Council there appeared a growing tendency to deal with the reform of religious Orders. St. Anthony Claret, who took part in Vatican I, has left us a set of notes which stress the decisive role of founders in the reform of their Institutes.[1] But Vatican I was unable to address this theme because it was interrupted by entrance of the Italian army into the City of Popes. It was addressed, however, although from a quite different point of view, by Vatican II, in various parts of the Dogmatic Constitution on the Church, *Lumen Gentium,* and in the decree *Perfectae Caritatis,* on the renewal and adaptation of the religious life. This has naturally brought with it a discussion of the same theme in various postconciliar documents issued by the Holy See.

We do not have the time to pick through the references to founders that are scattered throughout papal statements in recent years. This would involve going through the ample documentation contained in the *Acta Apostolicae Sedis* and *L'Osservatore Romano.* But speaking in general terms, we can say that recent popes have referred:

a) to the mission of each founder in the Church;

b) even more frequently, to their holiness;

c) to the permanence of their spirit in their sons and daughters and in contemporary reality;

d) to the Rules or Constitutions they wrote for their respective families.[2]

But if we restrict ourselves to Church documents that deal with founders in general, we find that the following basic points stand out:

1) The first idea that receives particular stress is that of the *unique mission of founders.* They are the ones who present the Rules, Constitutions, or Statutes to the hierarchy of the Church for approval,[3] and they are also the ones who define the aims proper of their institutions.[4] Founders, then, are the source of a particular tradition in the Church, and their sons and daughters must draw their inspiration from them throughout history. The renewal of their religious life consists precisely in a return to the founder. This idea, which was already sketched out by Pius XII,[5] received definitive expression in the decree *Perfectae Caritatis*[6] and was insistently proposed by Paul VI.[7]

2) The Constitution *Lumen Gentium* seems to be referring to the *sanctity of founders,* when it calls them "illustrious men and women."[8] This theme, as we have already mentioned, continuously appears in the papal Magisterium. Paul VI, in *Evangelica Testificatio,*

expressly invites religious to follow the example of the holiness of their founders.[9] In several instances, the popes have alluded to the particular religious experience and doctrine of founders (e.g., Pius XI, in his allocution on Claret, on February 25, 1934).

3) Among the particular elements that characterize the mission of founders, these documents single out: a) their aims,[10] b) their spirit,[11] c) their charisms.[12]

4) Special stress is laid on the "inspiration of founders." The popes have frequently stated that founders acted under an inspiration or motion of the Divine Spirit. Paul III and Julius III stated that St. Ignatius Loyola and his companions were gathered together *"Spiritu Sancto affati"* (inspired by the Holy Spirit).[13] Pius VI, in 1791, was the first pope of modern times to state the general principle that the foundation of an Institute of evangelical life is always due to a special inspiration.[14] Pius IX repeatedly stated that founders act under divine inspiration,[15] an affirmation repeated by Pius XI in his letter *Unigenitus,* addressed to superiors general.[16] Later, we shall see that Vatican II returned to stress this same teaching.

III

The Grace of Spiritual Fruitfulness

1. Origin: a Person

Since the existence of founders is a phenomenon that appears in the Church, we must direct our attention to the history of the Church in order to discover just what it means to be a founder. Father Jerome Nadel, S. J., reflecting on the origin of various religious Orders, suggests this line of approaching the question when he writes: "Before all else, God calls a person."[1]

This is a splendid fact. Everything that these Orders (and we would add: Congregations, Societies, Institutes, Lay Associations) have been throughout history, all that they have accomplished, all of these things have their genesis in a call addressed by God to a Christian person: Pachomius, Basil, Augustine, Benedict and Scholastica, Francis and Clare, Dominic, Philip Neri, Ignatius, Teresa, Angela Merici, Vincent de Paul and Louise de Marillac, Francis de Sales and Jane de Chantal, Sophie Barat, Blessed de Mazenod, Anthony Mary Claret, Antonia Paris, Elizabeth Seton, Frances Cabrini, Jeanne de Matel, Isaac Hecker, Teresa Gerhardinger. (May the many spiritual sons and daughters forgive us for not citing them all.) Judging by

19

more recent history and by the number of Causes for Beatification that are now accumulating in Rome, this list will grow much longer in the near future.

Reading through these names and thinking of still others, our attention is called to two facts. In the first place, these personalities form a glorious dynasty in the history of sanctity. They have enriched the Church in an extraordinary way through their spirituality, their activities, and also, quite often, with their doctrine. This simple fact suggests that the vitality of a religious Institute depends on the spiritual fullness of the man or woman to whom they owe their existence in the Body of Christ.

In the second place, almost all Institutes of evangelical life begin with a group of disciples or companions who surround an exceptional personality. We were obliged to use the expression, "almost all Institutes," for two reasons:

a) There is at least one case in which the grace of a founder was received in common by a whole group: the seven founders of the Servites.

b) There is one Order, the Carmelites, whose origin cannot be precisely identified. Since the Carmelites have no known founder (or perhaps, like the Servites, they were founded by a first group of hermits), and since they were first established in the same location in which the prophet Elijah worked, this Order renewed the ancient eremitical tradition that regarded this prophet as the man of God who established this way of life. Remember with what affection and devotion St. Teresa refers to her "father Elijah."

The association of the initial group with the founder has successively taken on two different aspects in the course of history. In the monastic Orders which derive from the desert tradition, the primitive nucleus was made up of a group of disciples who surrounded a charismatic master. In describing their relationship to him, they lay special stress on the spiritual doctrine they learned from him. Starting with the Mendicant Orders, the first group appears as a gathering of companions of the founder. Although the founder's doctrine is by no means forgotten, the main stress is laid on communion in the same vocation and rule of life.

2. The Father and the Mother

These historical data relating to the extraordinary vitality of founders and to the profound influence they exerted on their followers, help us understand why founders are ordinarily referred to as father or mother. In the desert, the titles "apa" (abbot or papa) and "ama" (mama), were applied to men and women who, after coming through serious trials, had reached a high degree of spiritual maturity and had attracted a certain group of disciples. In the first cenobitical communities this spiritual paternity or maternity soon became institutionalized. Pachomius is the first known example of a founder, and hence he was called "father" in a special way. The members of his Congregation continued referring to his sanctity and his spiritual gifts, as had been done with reference to the celebrated anchorites of the past, but they began to add a new element: By means of Pachomius, God gave us the Rule, and it was Pachomius who gathered the Congregation together. If we go on to St. Benedict, we notice that there is not the centralized organization we observed among the Pachomians. The autonomous Benedictine monasteries are bound together by the common observance of the Rule, and hence a greater stress is placed on doctrine. The Patriarch of Western Monasticism is accorded this title because in his Rule he taught a spiritual doctrine and outlined a rule of life.

It is significant that it was during the twelfth century, in the very period when the religious life began to be diversified, that references to the paternity of founders began to be more frequent. The reason for this phenomenon seems to be that it was then that the various groups began to insist on their proper origins. Drawing their inspiration from the text of St. Paul, "I have begotten you in Christ Jesus by means of the Gospel,[2] monks began to refer to their founders as men and women who engendered them by means of a Gospel teaching. Aelred of Rievaulx applies this notion to St. Benedict;[3] an anonymous writer applies it to St. Odo, the founder of Cluny;[4] Godfrey of Auxerre applies it to St. Bernard.[5] Surprisingly enough, however, the same text had already been cited by the Pachomians with reference to their founder, some seven or eight centuries earlier![6] Later, allusions to 1 Corinthians 4:15 fell into disuse, probably because founders were not mainly conceived of as generators through the doctrine they taught. But even so, the idea of the paternity or maternity of founders continued as alive as ever.

3. The Founder's Grace

From all of the foregoing we are led to conclude that the grace that distinguishes a founder is that of a *special fruitfulness in the Church.* St. John of the Cross expresses this very opinion in a passage of the *Living Flame of Love* (which we will examine later), the gist of which is that the highest mystical graces are reserved for founders, in proportion to the number of spiritual sons and daughters they are to have.[7] Father Jerome Nadal, S. J., whom we cited above, repeats the same idea:

> When God wishes to help his Church, he first raises up a person and gives him a special grace and a motion under which he must serve him in a special way. This is what He did with St. Francis: He gave him a particular grace both for his personal advancement and for that of his companions. . . . In the same way he raised up Ignatius and gave him a gift, and through him, he gave it to us.[8]

In connection with this Father Nadal goes on to bring out three distinct points:

1) The diversity of graces which distinguishes the various religious Orders may be compared to the variety of graces communicated by the sacraments.[9]

2) Under the influence of this distinctive grace, the common Christian virtues receive distinctive nuances, are activated, and move in certain directions.[10]

3) Applying Paul's teaching in 1 Corinthians 12:11, Nadal adds that we may say that this variety of spiritual gifts is aimed at increasing the beauty and vigor of the Church.[11]

Most theologians today refuse to accept, as stated, Nadal's comparison between the graces that distinguish the various religious Orders and the differences that exist in the grace communicated by the various sacraments. The reason for not accepting Nadal's statement literally is the fact that, as St. Thomas Aquinas teaches, the different sacramental graces presuppose a modification in grace itself.[12] But we can accept the notion that the different vocations of different religious Orders presupposes different *actual* graces, aimed at helping religious fulfill their different missions in the Church. At any rate, Nadal made two significant affirmations:

a) There is a differentiation in common Christian spirituality, a differentiation that derives from the particular grace granted to each religious family. It is here that we must discover the very source of the diversity of the diverse schools of spirituality.

b) This particular grace was granted first to founders and then, through them, to their Institutes.

The first companions of some founders, and the theologians of the first or second generations of some Orders, were keenly conscious of the intense irradiation of life and spirit that emanated from their fathers and mothers. In connection with the Franciscans, we might cite Thomas of Celano and St. Bonaventure; in connection with the Jesuits, we might include Father Ribadaneyra. Even more than this, some founders have themselves been aware of their own paternity or maternity. This is clear in some women founders, with typically feminine traits. Jeanne Chézard de Matel, foundress of the Order of the Incarnate Word, felt associated, precisely because of her vocation as founder, with the choir of patriarchs of the Old and New Testaments.[13] She even felt as if pregnant with her religious family.[14] and experienced the sufferings and contradictions involved in their foundation as birthpangs.[15] But above all she felt toward all her daughters a strong sense of maternal love.[16]

This phenomenon had already figured in the life of St. Teresa of Jesus. She, too, had a deeply felt sense of motherhood toward her nuns. She knew that some of the graces the Lord had granted her were meant for them:

> My daughters must believe that it is for their own good that the Lord has enabled me to realize in some degree what blessings are to be found in holy poverty.[17]

As we follow the great Saint of Avila through the course of her successive writings, we can observe the steady growth of these maternal feelings. In the *Way of Perfection* (finished in 1564), she frequently calls them "my sisters" and "my friends," placing them so to speak on the same level as herself. Nevertheless, even in this work, especially when she wants to make an important exhortation regarding the religious life of her nuns, she immediately shifts into the expression "daughters" or "my daughters."[18] In the *Foundations* (begun years later, in 1573) and in her letters, Teresa always addresses them as "my daughters."

In her letters Catherine McAuley expresses deep tenderness for her sisters, whom she sometimes calls "my dear child." To one of her sisters who is absent, she writes: "How anxiously I long to be with you." "Give my most affectionate love to my dear Sr. Chantal, Sr. Genevieve. . . ." She frequently adds: "Write me soon"[19] St. Micaela of the Blessed Sacrament also felt a lively love for her sisters.

It remains for us to define in what this founder's grace consists— this grace which makes foundresses and founders spiritually fruitful in the Church.

IV

The Founding Charism

In discussing the gift of spiritual fruitfulness that is proper to founders, Father Nadal had recourse to the teaching of Paul in First Corinthians on the different graces granted for the strength and vigor of the whole Body, adding that there are "particular graces" that are granted to the various religious families, for the good of the whole Church. This sets us squarely in the midst of the theology of charisms, although the good sixteenth-century Jesuit did not use this technical term derived from Greek. In our times, however, this term is used with increasing frequency to explain the differences which exist between the various Institutes of evangelical life. Thus, we speak of the charism of founders and the charism of a community. Since this word, *charism,* expresses a well-defined category of realities, we should by all means ask in what sense it can be applied to the religious life.

1. The Charisms of the Religious Life in the Magisterium

The Second Vatican Council, in its documents on the religious life, frequently uses the Latin term, *donum* (the equivalent of the Greek term, *charisma*). In two of the Council documents, *donum* is used to explain the nature of celibacy, citing Matthew 19:11 and 1 Corinthians 7:7 in this connection.[1] We would expect such a reference in the Dogmatic Constitution on the Church. But in the very next number of this Constitution, the Council broadens this category to include all of the "counsels" professed by religious.[2] For this reason the Church's pastors have, with regard to the counsels, certain rights and duties similar to those they have with regard to the charisms granted by the Spirit. If the mission of these pastors with regard to charisms in general is to discern them and regulate their practice (in imitation of what Paul did in his Churches), Vatican II goes on to affirm that these same pastors have a twofold mission with regard to the evangelical counsels, namely, "to give a right interpretation of the counsels and to regulate their practice."[3] Notice the difference in the latter case: Pastors are not to discern, but to interpret, since the evangelical counsels have already been discerned, identified, and acknowledged throughout a long ecclesiastical tradition.

Note, too—although we do not have the space or time to demonstrate it here—that the category of *charism* was the first one that the Fathers, starting with Origen, applied to the whole area of what soon came to be called *consilium* (counsel). And this procedure has an obvious New Testament basis in the texts quoted by Vatican II in connection with celibacy, especially in 1 Corinthians 7:7. Since the "counsels" are the most typical characteristic of the religious life, defining the charisms is equivalent to saying that the religious life is in itself a charism of the Spirit.

This puts us in the context of the theology of the religious life in general. More to our point, it touches upon the object of our study of the spiritual doctrine concerning founders. In this connection the crucial question we might ask is this: To what extent and in what sense can the differences between the various Institutes of the religious life be explained on the basis of a particular charism received by each founder and in some way transmitted through the founder to his or her family?

We should observe that the Council never explicitly uses the expression, "the charism of founders." Nevertheless, in describing the appearance of the phenomenon of the religious life in the Church, it mentions the "wonderful variety" *(mirabilis varietas)* of religious Institutes and several times uses the words *dona* and *donationes* (gifts), always with express reference to St. Paul's doctrine on the many spiritual gifts that contribute to the upbuilding of the one

Body. Thus, it speaks of the various gifts *(variis donis)*[4] and a great variety of gifts *(tanta donorum varietate)*[5] involved in the religious life. Later, in number 8 of *Perfectae Caritatis,* dealing with the great number of apostolic communities, the Council again refers to the "gifts which vary according to the grace that is given" to each of these families *(donationes secundum gratiam quae data est eis).*[6] In other words, in order to explain this phenomenon of the *variety* of the religious life, the Council has had recourse to the doctrine of St. Paul on the variety of members in the same Body and, more concretely, it has chosen to use Paul's terminology relating to the "various gifts" of the Spirit, i.e., to the charisms. One might object that, in number 1 of *Perfectae Caritatis,* the Council cites Ephesians 4:12, that is, a text in which the word *dona,* and not *charismata,* is used in order to describe the various gifts which enrich the Church. Doesn't this show that when the Council used the word *donum* to describe the variety of gifts which distinguish religious Institutes, it wanted to give *donum* a broader, nontechnical meaning? The answer is a simple *no:* The objection is unfounded. In fact, it should be noted that the Council, even in this same initial paragraph, refers to Paul's teaching on the Body of Christ and calls the "gifts" referred to as *spiritualia,* i.e., derived from the Spirit. But above all it should be noted that in number 8 of the same decree, the Council expressly cites Romans 12 and 1 Corinthians 12, the two classic Pauline texts on *charisms* in the Church. The Second Vatican Council has clearly used the category of charism in order to explain the variety of Institutes of evangelical life among the People of God.

Paul VI insistently harked back to this Council teaching. He did this mainly in his exhortation, *Evangelica Testificatio,* where he used the word *charism* to refer to the distinctive graces of founders:

> Only in this way will you be able to arouse people's hearts to embrace the divine truth and love according to the *charisms of your founders,* whom God raised up in his Church. In no other way does the Council rightly insist that religious of both sexes have the duty of faithfully preserving the spirit of their originators, the way these persons presented the Gospels, and their example of holiness. Religious must recognize here one of the fundamentals for achieving present-day renewal, and one of the most certain norms for deciding what kind of activity each Institute should undertake.[7]

The Pope does no more here than to repeat the doctrine of the Council in greater depth and detail. Above all, however, this text launches a new expression—"the charism of founders"—which was to enjoy a great vogue from that time on. Note that this was not the first time he used this expression. At least one time before this he used the same terms in the same context: He had spoken to the sons of St. Louis Grignion de Montfort on the charism of their father, in March of 1969.[8] After the publication of *Evangelica Testificatio*, he continued to use this expression. In his visit to the monastery of Subiaco, on September 8, 1971, he told the Benedictines that they "were guided by the charism of an inspired and excellent interpreter of the Lord's ways."[9] Shortly thereafter he told the Passionist sisters: "You have made your own the charism of St. Paul of the Cross: that of being living witness of the Lord's Passion."[10] He wrote to the superior general of the Congregation of St. Joseph of Murialdo, that the members of that Institute were "heirs to the charism" of St. Leonard Murialdo.[11] Finally, at the canonization of St. Teresa Jornet, Paul VI spoke of the charism granted to this Saint.[12]

John Paul II has continued this line of thought, begun by his predecessor, by stressing the need of respect for the variety of charisms of religious Institutes, and by recommending that their members maintain fidelity to this charism.

Above all, the Pope has reaffirmed the existence of these distinctive charisms at the very origin of each religious family:

> Each of your founders, under the inspiration of the Holy Spirit promised by Christ to his Church, was a man who possessed a particular charism. Christ had in him an exceptional instrument for his work of salvation, which, especially in this way, is perpetuated in the history of the human family. The Church has gradually assumed these charisms, evaluated them, and when she found them authentic, thanked the Lord for them and tried to put them in a safe place in the life of the community so that they could always yield fruit.[13]

These charisms of founders and foundresses are manifold. The Church, as the Pope states elsewhere, needs this variety of charisms and vocations, since both its spiritual richness and its service to humanity depend on it.[14]

Hence, the Pope recommends fidelity to these foundational charisms. He insisted on this in the discourse he delivered at Loyola to the major superiors of Institutes of Spanish origin:

> The fact is that charisms of founders must remain in the communities to which they gave rise. The charism ought to constitute the principle of the life of each religious family at all times.[15]

Among the latest Vatican documents dealing with the religious life there is one which dwells expressly on the charism of founders as transmitted to their disciples. *Mutuae Relationes* was jointly published by the Congregation of Bishops and the Congregation for Religious and Secular Institutes on May 14, 1978:

> There are many religious Institutes in the Church, each differing from the other according to its proper character (cf. PC 7, 8, 9, 10). Each, however, contributes its own vocation as a gift raised up by the Spirit through the work of outstanding men and women (cf. LG 45; PC 1, 2), and authentically approved by the sacred hierarchy.
>
> The very charism of the founders (EN 11) appears as "an experience of the Spirit" transmitted to their disciples to be lived, safeguarded, deepened and constantly developed by them, in harmony with the body of Christ continually in the process of growth. "It is for this reason that the distinctive character of various religious Institutes is preserved and fostered by the Church" (LG 44; cf. CD 33, 35.1, 35.2, etc.). This distinctive character also involves a particular style of sanctification and apostolate, which creates its particular tradition, with the result that one can readily perceive its objective elements.[16]

This text is significant for several reasons. In the first place, it shows the extent to which the term "charism" is coming into common, and in some sense official, use, in order to explain the identity (and correlative diversity) of the various religious Institutes in the Church. In the second place, this text takes as its starting point the Second Vatican Council's explanation of the various forms of religious life, based ultimately on St. Paul's teaching on charisms. Finally, this text further develops this thought by amplifying it with various aspects emerging from current theological reflection: 1) the founding charism is an experience of the Spirit granted to the founder or foundress; 2) this charism is a reality to be transmitted and safeguarded but also a dynamic reality to be constantly deepened and developed; 3) this charism encompasses a type of spirituality and apostolate which, in turn, gives rise to a special tradition.

Important as this text is, it does not of course clarify all aspects of the founding charism. In fact, a reading of the text gives rise to a number of questions—questions that we will attempt to address in their proper context in what follows.

2. Uses of the Word "Charism"

The repeated references in Council documents to Pauline teaching on charisms, as well as Paul VI's precise use of the term, indicates that the Church has given the term *charism* a well-defined meaning in its doctrine on the religious life and its varied forms. Unfortunately, as we all know the constant use and abuse of this term in contemporary theological jargon tends to dull its contours and make its meaning all too vague.

In citing these Pauline texts on charisms, Scholasticism used to speak of graces *gratis datae* (gratuitously given), in contradistinction to grace *gratum faciens* (making gracious or pleasing, namely, to God). *Gratia gratum faciens*—justifying or sanctifying grace—is given to unite a human being with God, while the various *gratiae* (graces) *gratis datae* are given in order to help us cooperate better with God in the salvation or justification of others.[17] St. Thomas Aquinas, with his typical fidelity to the text of Scripture, believed that all of these latter kinds of graces are encompassed in Paul's enumeration in 1 Corinthians 12:8-10.[18] From the Council of Trent onward this terminology came to be accepted in spiritual theology with the same meaning attached to it by St. Thomas: "gifts of the Holy Spirit that are not necessarily related to the development of Christian life and, hence, not infused with justifying grace in Baptism, nor communicated through some other sacrament, but rather granted by God to certain persons for the good of the whole Church."[19]

As time passed two suppositions began to infiltrate this common doctrine. In the first place, there arose the notion that the charisms Paul speaks of were related in a privileged or even exclusive way to the primitive Church.[20] This is surely not the meaning Paul attaches to them. For not only does Paul not relate charisms to the apostolic or foundational phase of the Church, but he tends to view the Church in its eschatological dimension.[21] This tendency to reduce charisms to "privileges of the apostolic Church" partly explains why, contrary to the thought of Aquinas, they had so little influence in ecclesiology.

In the second place, by reading only some of the texts of St. Paul a number of people came to believe that the category of charisms in the New Testament referred only to such extraordinary phenomena as revelations, prophecies, speaking in tongues, and healing. This explains why, in the past, charisms were mentioned exclusively by theologians of spirituality and why, at present, they appear in the language of the "charismatic" or neo-pentecostalist movement.

Obviously, when Paul VI and other people concerned with the theology of the religious life speak of the charism of a founder or an Institute they use the term in a broader sense. In view of these different meanings attached to "charism," it is necessary to investigate what the New Testament tells us on this point.

3. Charism in the New Testament

The word *charisma,* which is missing in the Greek version of the Old Testament and very rare in the writings of the Apostolic Fathers,[22] is found seventeen times in the New Testament, all, with the sole exception of 1 Peter 4:10, in the Letters of St. Paul. The primary meaning of charism is "grace" (Gk., *charis*) and hence in one case can mean "the grace of having escaped from the danger of death" (2 Cor. 1:9) or, in a group of texts, it means the grace granted to all in justification, that is, justifying grace.[23] In Romans 11:29 the term signifies all of the gifts granted to Israel, gifts that can be summed up in Israel's vocation *(klēsis).*[24]

With the exception of 2 Corinthians 1:9, we have thus far been speaking in the context of the grace granted by God to his people in the Old and New Testaments. But there is another series of texts that speak of the different gifts granted to different members of the Church. Here, the term "charism" tends to be used in a technical sense. Among these texts, only one of them uses charism to designate a type of Christian existence, namely, celibacy/matrimony: "Each has his own special *gift* from God, one of one kind and one of another" (1 Cor. 7:7). Here, charism obviously signifies a permanent grace, identifiable with a personal vocation. In all of the other texts, charism is always related to a ministry *(diakonia)* or to an activity *(energema):*

—According to 1 Corinthians 12:8-11, a charism may be not only the ability to heal, to perform miracles, to discern, to speak in tongues or interpret them, but also the distinctive gifts of a preacher or teacher.

—In the list given in 1 Corinthians 12:28-30, a charism may be the distinctive gift of an apostle, a prophet, a teacher, a helper, or an administrator, as well as that of a healer, a wonder-worker, a speaker in tongues, or an interpreter of tongues.

—In Romans 12:6-8, the charisms mentioned are prophecy, service, teaching, exhortation, almsgiving, governance, and works of mercy.

—In Ephesians 4:11-13, the gifts (not called *charismata,* but rather *donata*) are those of apostles, prophets, evangelizers, pastors, and teachers; in other words, the various sorts of ecclesiastical offices.

Because of some of the gifts mentioned in 1 Corinthians 12, especially those relating to an enthusiastic way of understanding and living within the Church, it came to be supposed that St. Paul, in speaking of charisms, was referring to transitory manifestations of the Spirit. Moreover it is clear that the teaching of St. Paul does take into account the possibility of certain extraordinary outpourings of the Spirit on some Christians. But Paul's attention tends to focus on gifts that define a Christian's position in the Church, and that are therefore permanent. In the pneumatic ecclesiology of First Corinthians, these "extraordinary" gifts are ordinary. In Romans 12 and Ephesians 4, only permanent gifts connected with ecclesiastical offices are mentioned. As E. Bettencourt has pointed out, Paul clearly is making an effort to separate the charisms from the sphere of pure religious enthusiasm.[25]

We may conclude, then, that the term "charism," as used in those

New Testament texts that refer to various gifts received by Christians, signifies a "gift granted to a person by the Spirit for the common upbuilding of the Church." Although it does not exclude occasional manifestations of the Spirit, charism tends to appear as a permanent gift which shapes the vocation of a Christian within the fold of the Church. In general, St. Paul relates charisms to various ministerial activities and, finally, with duties or offices in the Church. But a charism can also be a vocation to a type of Christian life, such as celibacy or matrimony (1 Cor. 7:7). In the Pastoral Letters, the charisms appear as closely linked to ecclesiastical offices and are communicated through the laying on of hands (1 Tm. 4:14, 2 Tm. 1:6). The process of institutionalization is obvious.

Summing up these data on the different gifts granted to different members of the People of God, we would offer the following conclusions:

1) The charisms form part of a pneumatic vision of Church: It is the Holy Spirit who distributes them (1 Cor. 12:1; 4; 11; 12).

2) The charisms are given for the common good of the Church; that is, they facilitate personal cooperation in the common upbuilding of the Body of Christ. The category "charism" is profoundly ecclesial. 1 Peter 4:10, the only non-Pauline text to use this term, reminds us of the community orientation of charisms.

3) Originally, a charism is not a ministry or an activity, but rather a grace whereby the Spirit makes a person apt for some ministry. But gradually, since charisms are known only through activities, they come to be identified with activities. From the moment charisms become related with ecclesiastical offices, they tend to be identified with a vocation. This is the sense given to charisms in 1 Corinthians 7:7 when it refers to celibacy/matrimony. We should also note that St. Paul himself, in Romans 11:29, associates the concept of charism with that of vocation, albeit the vocation of Israel.

4. Charisms and Religious Life

Bearing in mind the meaning attached to the word "charism" in the Pauline texts and First Peter that refer to the different graces received by different members of the People of God, we should note the close coincidence between the New Testament meaning of the term and that given it recently in statements of the Magisterium concerning the various gifts which characterize the religious life, the gifts or charisms proper to the various forms of the religious life, or the gifts or charisms of founders and their Institutes.

If charism is understood as a gift of the Spirit associated with a vocation to a type of life (1 Cor. 7:7) or with a ministry in the Church (1 Cor. 12; Rm. 12; Eph. 4), the Council obviously deals with this when, echoing an ancient tradition, it speaks of celibacy and the other counsels as *dona* (gifts). This is also true of those cases where Vatican II, followed by Pope Paul VI, uses the term *donum* and *charisma* to refer to the graces of the Spirit which characterize the various forms of religious life in different religious Institutes. These charisms are gifts granted for the good of the whole Church and determine the existential situation of a religious individual or group within the Body of Christ. They are gifts which, as Aquinas says, speaking of graces *gratis datae,* are mainly *(potius)* ordered toward the whole Church,[26] but it is also clear that at the same time they determine the way in which one or more individuals are to grow in the life of Christ. The one aspect is inseparable from the other.[27]

Later we shall attempt to describe more precisely the elements that constitute a founder's charism, and we shall try to see how and to what extent this charism is transmitted to his or her sons or daughters. Before this, however, we should examine the way in which founders discover their vocation, that is, the way in which they become aware of the charism that has been granted to them. Then we should study each of the data that are usually repeated in the lives of founders, in order at last to be able to judge which of them are passed on to their successors as elements that belong to the community charism.

Before going any further we would like to respond to an objection which is occasionally heard. It has been said that "when, in reference to an Institute, the word *charism* is used, the term is not taken in its proper sense. A charism is a passing and particularly gratuitous experience of the Holy Spirit's action. It is not a grace of state."[28] We would like to register our dissent with this opinion. As we have already observed in St. Paul, charism does not merely refer to "passing experiences," but also and ever more increasingly in successive texts indicates gifts of the Spirit which make it possible to carry out different ministries or adopt different lifestyles in the Church. The term *charism* is therefore used in its proper Pauline sense when it is regarded as a vocational gift which the Spirit gives to each member of the Institute and which coincides essentially with the gift originally received by the founder or foundress. On the problem that arises from our use of the term *transmission* in this case, we will devote some considerations later in this study.

V

The Original Inspiration

In citing Father Jerome Nadal, S.J., we encountered the insight that the history of almost all religious families begins with the call of a single Christian, which then becomes a calling or vocation of a whole group. We then cited documents in which the popes, speaking either of a particular founder or of founders in general, have attributed the foundation of a religious Institutes to an inspiration whereby the Holy Spirit enlightened their founders. In doing so the popes have only added their support to an idea that appeared very early in the history of the religious life.

1. The Action of God

While St. Athanasius' *Vita Antonii* narrates the vocation of the great anchorite as the vocation of an individual (although he is seen as a model for others),[1] the biographers of St. Pachomius show how their protagonist, under the influence of successive graces, discovered both his own vocation and the rule of life of his Congregation. First, they relate how at his very Baptism a ray of light struck one of his hands and then spread from his hand onto the floor, from which it continued to cover the whole earth.[2] Later, they tell us, an angel revealed to him that God willed him to spend his life serving his neighbors, and how Pachomius then proceeded to build a series of cells surrounded by a common wall for his future disciples.[3] Palladius, in his *Historia Lausiaca,* states that a Rule which he attributed to Pachomius had been dictated to him by an angel.[4]

Interestingly, neither Basil nor Augustine nor Benedict mention a particular motion or light from God in connection with the gathering together of their first companions. In contrast, St. Francis of Assisi is perhaps the father of a religious family who most clearly attributes his action to a divine inspiration. In his *Testament* he states:

> And after the Lord gave me friars, no one was teaching me what I ought to do. But the Most High himself revealed to me that I should live according to the form of the Holy Gospel. And I, in few and simple words, caused it to be written down, and the lord Pope confirmed it for me.[5]

St. Paul of the Cross, too, uses the term inspiration to describe first his personal inclination to solitude and then his vocation to gather companions "who would live together in unity to promote the fear of God in souls."[6]

We find something similar in the lives of other foundresses or founders. But it is better for us to cite some of them when we come to study the different modes in which this action of the Spirit took place.

Let us state for the present, in a preliminary way, that even before they discovered their vocation founders and foundresses were prepared for it by graces that disposed them. This process of gradual and intense preparation is visible in St. Francis of Assisi, St. Ignatius of Loyola (Manresa), and in St. Paul of the Cross. The childhood and youth of Anthony Claret were enlivened by a series of pedagogical graces.[7] Before Mother Maria Kaupas began the journey to Switzerland and the United States which would eventually lead her to found the Sisters of Saint Casimir, she received some spiritual experiences that fortified and enriched her spirit during a visit to the Shrine of our Lady of Vilnius.[8]

2. Various Modes of Inspiration

There have been cases in which the inspiration whereby the Saints and Servants of God discovered their vocation seems to have been granted by way of some extraordinary phenomenon: a vision, a divine locution, or some special illumination of their mind. In these cases we may speak of a revelation.

We cannot be totally sure of the historic value of the events referred to in the various *Lives* of St. Pachomius, and there are abundant reasons for rejecting Palladius' legend of an angel dictating a Rule to Pachomius. In contrast, there is no reason to doubt the authenticity of the exalted religious experiences which moved St. Francis of Assisi to adopt his form of life. The words of the *Testament* seem, indeed, to refer to a divine action that was not circumscribed to a determined moment, but rather to one that may have taken place over a long period of time. Nevertheless, the Saint clearly presents himself as having been illumined in this by God. The *Lives* of Francis speak of a locution through which the Lord entrusted the Saint with the mission of rebuilding his house, and they recount the profound impression produced in Francis by his reading of the Mission Charge in the Gospels.[9]

Of St. Ignatius Loyola we know the intense mystical experiences he enjoyed at Manresa, which Father Ribadeneyra rightly associates with the foundation of the Society of Jesus,[10] as well as the vision he was graced with at La Storta.[11] Jeanne Chézard de Matel discovered her vocation to found the Order of the Incarnate Word in a series of mystical experiences which virtually inundated her during a few days in August, 1620. Grace continued to enlighten her periodically with symbolic visions relating to her spiritual family.[12] The decision to found the Passionists was the result of a succession of mystical experiences granted to St. Paul of the Cross[13] Anthony Mary Claret has told us how he discovered his apostolic vocation through the extraordinary lights and movements that he received while reading the Bible.[14] Father Lamy, founder of the Servants of Jesus and Mary,[15] and Mother Magdalen of the Incarnation, founder of the Sisters of Perpetual Adoration,[16] had express revelations that God willed them to be, respectively, the father and mother of new religious families. Mother Antonia Paris who, together with St. Anthony Mary Claret, founded the Claretian Sisters, was favored by particularly strong prophetic enlightenments.[17]

Legends have often grown up around the theme of founders discovering their vocation. We have already noted that Palladius' account of the angel dictating the Rule to Pachomius is devoid of historical foundation. But since the Rule was the central element in monastic life, this was considered an appropriate way of expressing the conviction that the founding of the Pachomian Congregation was the outcome of a divine revelation. Much later, toward the end of the Middle Ages, when the various habits came to be regarded as symbols of different Orders, the collective imagination of the religious who belonged to them created a series of "histories" in which Christ, or often the Blessed Virgin, appear in a vision granting the habit to the founder or, in the case of the Blessed Virgin, wearing this habit. Here, in a different form corresponding to a different cultural context, we have an expression of the same conviction concerning the supernatural origin of the Institute. But both the earlier and later forms of the legend point to a reality born under the influence of a particular grace. It is curious to note that although the giving of an Institute's habit by Christ or the Blessed Virgin first arose in later legends as a literary form of saying that there was a divine intervention in the founding of these Institutes, these legends seem to have been so influential with still later founders that they came to have imaginary visions of the future habit their own Institutes would wear. This is not an argument against the authenticity of these visions and experiences, since we are dealing here with paramystical phenomena which are produced in the human imagination and are hence subject to the influence of their recipient's environment as to the form they take. Jeanne Chézard de Matel had a whole series of sensible visions in which she saw the emblem and habit of her Order of the Incarnate Word.[18] St. Paul of the Cross also had a vision in which he saw the Blessed Virgin clothed in the Passionist habit.[19]

There are other cases in which the discovery is not made within the context of an extraordinary phenomenon, although it could be said that it came through a particularly intense light which left a great sense of certainty. Here we are fully within the world of mystical experience. St. Bartolomea Capitanio, who founded the Sisters of Charity, felt within herself a strong impulse to outline the future shape of her Institute.[20] Narrating the way in which the traits of her Congregation kept emerging in her mind, the Saint repeats:

> I believe that it was during a Communion when I had this thought. Another time, I believe it was at prayer, I had this thought. . . . On another occasion, while I was working, I had this thought, which was

confirmed for me in various Communions and at prayer. . . . This thought of the imitation of the Redeemer, etc., that I have had with such clarity that I can't explain it, and I seemed to see the beauty and sweetness of the Rules conductive to that aim. . . . I cannot rid my heart of the conviction that Jesus wants this new family. . . . I cannot pass over in silence, the fact that I seem to have felt most sensibly in my heart that. . . .[21]

This is why so many founders have attributed the work they have carried out to God.

When a revelation of this sort is transmitted by way of an extraordinary phenomenon, the vocational discovery may come in a sudden flash of awareness. But even in this case it is frequently the outcome of a longer process. This is how it ordinarily happens: The Saints and Servants of God gradually become aware of the fact of their being called by God to establish a new religious group in the Church. Enlightenment comes to them in prayer, in reflection, in dialogue with others, and in taking counsel with others. Of course, this process evolves at least under the ordinary graces of the Spirit: Divine light draws their attention to determined needs in the Church, while an inner impulse moves their wills to offer themselves to God as instruments.

But it is one thing for a founder or foundress to discover his or her own vocation to a certain style of life or ministry in the Church and quite another for them to understand that it is God's will that they found a religious Institute. There is ordinarily some time lag between the first step and the second. But even when they have taken their second step, founder's usually do all they can to discern whether it is really God's will. Father Thaddeus Grzeszczyk describes two cases relevant to this point. The first involves Mother Marie-Anne, the founder of the Sisters of St. Anne of Montreal. At twenty-two years of age she already understood the need for a Congregation dedicated to the apostolate among young women and felt called to this work. Nevertheless, she kept this to herself for a whole year, praying and reflecting on it until she could do so no longer. Then she informed the bishop of Montreal of the matter.[22] The second case refers to Father Benito Menni, O.H. He did all that he could to reject the idea of founding a Congregation of sisters dedicated to the care of mentally ill women, and even strove to dissuade the first two pious women who wanted to do this work. The perseverance of these two holy women, despite the trials and obstacles he put in their way, finally convinced him that this work was God's will, and so he gave in to it.[23] Thus, the Hospital Sisters of the Sacred Heart of Jesus came into being.

The record of history shows that founders ordinarily went through a long process before deciding to found their Institute, and an even longer process before defining all of the characteristic traits of these Institutes. This has been true even of those cases in which an extraordinary experience was involved. St. Francis of Assisi heard the crucified Lord ask him to rebuild his house (the Church). Francis began by rebuilding the little church of San Damiano. St. Ignatius Loyola shows us in his diary how much he had to pray and reflect before taking some important decisions on the nature of the Society of Jesus. Father Jerome Nadal adverts to the fact:

> Ordinarily, God prepared and educates founders, gradually impressing on their hearts the idea of their future Congregation, helping them discover in their own lives what they will subsequently propose to the others. This is what happened with St. Ignatius.[24]

This explains the fact that religious Institutes are frequently formed in a gradual way and, in some cases, their final form is preceded by an experience of some nondefinitive kind of association. In the Society of Jesus the first group already had a commitment of association as early as 1534 (the promise of Montmartre), but the decision to found a religious Order was not made until the encounters held in Rome in 1539. St. Vincent de Paul was moved by the situation prevailing in the rural areas and felt the need to evangelize them. First he obtained funds from his patroness, Mme de Gondi, and then strove to procure the services of some Jesuits or Oratorians. When his attempt failed, Mme de Gondi forced his hand by having her brother-in-law, the Archbishop of Paris appoint him rector of a school where he could gather and form missionary priests. The Congregation of the Mission thus began to loom on the horizon.[25] Catherine McAuley began with a Mercy House (1827), followed it with the foundation of a lay association (1827), and ended by founding a Congregation of sisters (1830). St. Anthony Claret went through a whole series of phases, starting from a period of personal ministry

(1839), to an open group of companions (1842), to a Congregation of priests and brothers (1849), to a Congregation of simple vows (1870—the year of his death).[26]

The case of Isaac Thomas Hecker is somewhat unusual, although it involves a number of aspects frequently repeated in the course of history. He, too, discovered his vocation to create a new religious family as the result of a process attended by unexpected circumstances. Shortly after joining the Catholic Church, Hecker, who came from a fervent Methodist background, began to feel urged by a desire to work for the salvation of the American people. Eventually he came to see the need for a religious community specifically committed to that purpose, although at the time he hardly suspected that he might be called upon to found one. Like a few other founders and a good many foundresses, he first entered another Institute: the Redemptorists. But, like other founders who entered other Institutes, after a few years he discovered that his path seemed to be leading in a different direction. Hecker was launched on his new path in a rather traumatic way: He was expelled from the Redemptorists. He appealed to a Roman cardinal, who suggested that he himself should start an American community. Soon afterwards, Hecker founded the Congregation of the Missionary Priests of St. Paul the Apostle.

This fact of the gradual discovery of their vocation by founders and foundresses appears in history with impressive clarity and frequency. We have already seen how Francis of Assisi kept groping until the light of grace illumined him completely. Ignatius, too, kept searching for God's will until the famous meeting at the Pincio, when he and his companions decided to establish a religious Order. Even after this, the Saint continued questioning the Lord on important aspects of the rule of life for the Society, such as poverty. Anthony Claret went through a whole series of phases. Even after receiving his first inspiration to go to solitude and to live a life of poverty. Paul of the Cross confesses: "I did not know what God wanted of me, so for this reason I did not think of it further." The Saint shows how his calling emerged gradually: an inspiration to withdraw into solitude, an inspiration to gather companions, to promote the fear of God in souls, a vision in which he received the habit, a stronger compelling desire to gather companions, after which "God infused into my soul in a lasting manner the form of the holy Rule to be observed."[27]

In the apostolic Congregations, the first element of the charism to appear is an awareness of some vital need in the Church and the call to respond to that need. Jean-Baptiste de la Salle, Nano Nagle, Edmund Rice, and Theresa Gerhardinger all began by founding a school and ended up establishing an Institute. Nano Nagle and Micaela of the Blessed Sacrament first entrusted their centers to an already existing Congregation, without becoming personally involved or committed, until they finally faced the evidence that God wanted their personal commitment. Jean-Baptiste de la Salle felt a pronounced repugnance for becoming personally involved in "charity schools," until he realized that this was God's will for him. Micaela of the Blessed Sacrament also seems to have experienced a somewhat similar feeling. There is, then, frequently a series of tentative steps and even some resistance on the part of many founders and foundresses: Like Jonah, these prophets, too, try to escape their call until the divine light deeply illumines them.

3. Inspiration and Prophetic Mission

The popes, in attributing a special inspiration to founders, seem to have compared them in some way with the prophets. Indeed, inspiration is a characteristic element of the prophetic spirit. In the same vein, the Second Vatican Council, in the dogmatic constitution *Lumen Gentium,* has described the attitude of the hierarchy vis-à-vis founders in terms that seem to attribute to the latter a prophetic mission in the Church:

> Again, in docile response to the promptings of the Holy Spirit, the hierarchy accepts rules of religious life which are presented for its approval by outstanding men and women, authentically approves them after reviewing them, and uses its supervisory and protective authority to ensure that religious Institutes established throughout the world for the upbuilding of the Body of Christ may develop and flourish in accordance with the spirit of their founders.[28]

It should be noted that this is exactly the way in which *Lumen Gentium* describes the attitude of the hierarchy with regard to the charisms of the prophetic spirit, an attitude of: discerning them, judging their authenticity, and formulating rules for their appropriate use.[29]

In truth, inspiration is not the only trait that founders have in common with prophets. In stating that founders were "raised up by God in his Church," Paul VI suggested that they received a special mission from God. And "mission" is also a distinctive trait of prophets.

In order to understand this attribution of a prophetic spirit to the Saints and Servants of God who have created new religious families, it should be borne in mind that, contrary to what is commonly thought and taken as obvious, a prophet is not just a man or woman who makes predictions. As biblical theologians and exegetes have been telling us for decades, a prophet is not necessarily one who *foretells* certain future events, but is mainly one who stands in the place of God and *forth-tells (prophemi)* God's will in a message to God's People. St. Cyril of Jerusalem saw very clearly (although somewhat narrowly) that the prophetic spirit presupposes a supernatural and deep knowledge of history.[30] This is true, not because (as Cyril believed) Moses wrote the history of humankind from Adam to the entry into the promised land, but because the prophets were in fact instruments through which God intervened in history. Their message was meant to illumine and change the course of history, and hence presupposed a deep knowledge and sense of contemporary historic events. In not a few cases the prophets strove to confront the present situation by contrasting it with the purity of the chosen people's origins and by preaching a return to those origins. This was particularly true of Elijah, Amos, and the Deuteronomistic School.

To a greater or lesser extent, this is precisely what the various founders have done. Gregory IX, in the bull of canonization of St. Dominic, wrote that the Saint had been "raised up by God" (again, a prophetic expression) to help the Church in a moment of acute crisis.[31] God's "raising up" of founders as a way of responding to certain problems affecting the Church in one period is a notion frequently expressed in pontifical documents. We can likewise find it outside the papal Magisterium, in the tradition of the religious life itself. To cite but one case, St. Anthony Mary Claret twice refers in his writings to the fact that founders have been "sent or raised up by God" in order to provide a remedy for some urgent needs of his people.[32] Here we begin to touch the heart of the question. On the basis of the data we have seen, we can state that the inspiration received by founders has two immediate objectives: on the one hand,

the historical situation of the Church in the founders' lifetime, especially with relation to the Church's pressing needs; on the other, the
need to return to the Gospel and the way in which this is to be done
(return to the sources).

Even the most summary review of the history of the Church would
lead us to the conclusion that the *new forms of religious life* are born
as a result of a *return to the Gospel (sine glossa,* without additional
compromising commentary) during a period when the Church is
undergoing powerful pressures. St. Basil and St. Francis both speak
expressly of living faithfully according to the Gospel, that is, of
getting back to it. In Charles de Foucauld the immediacy and the
freshness of this Gospel spirit is equally visible. St. Pachomius and St.
Augustine, and later the whole Benedictine tradition, sought to incarnate in their communities the spirit of the primitive Church of
Jerusalem. All of them somehow wanted to reincarnate Christian
origins. This movement of a return to the Gospel is implicit in such
wide-ranging works as those of St. Benedict and St. Ignatius Loyola.

New forms of religious life are also born as a *response to a crisis in
the Church.* This is one of the most surprising facts in the history of
religious Institutes. Without falling into facile and superficial general-
izations, let us recall just a few parallels: the flight to the desert, in
contraposition to the established Church of Constantine; the Basilian
fraternity, in contraposition to the secularism of bishops and the
puritanism of the various ascetical movements in Asia Minor; Benedictine monasticism, in contraposition to the barbarian invasions; St.
Francis and St. Dominic, in response to an evolving society, to Albi-
gensianism and to the various poverty movements in the Middle
Ages; St. Ignatius Loyola, in response to the discovery of the New
World and to the Protestant Reformation.[33]

By this we do not pretend to imply that every founder or foundress
had a detailed vision of the forces and tendencies at work in his or
her society. But it must be said that they never made their decision to
found an Order merely as the result of an intellectual process. An
inspiration always retains its character as an instinctual kind of ap-
prehension. In dealing with the gifts of the Holy Spirit, St. Thomas
Aquinas explains "inspiration" as being moved by a sort of "divine
instinct."[34] But even if this is generally so, we cannot rule out the role
played by consciousness in this overall process of inspiration. St.
Teresa of Avila expressly mentions divisions among Christians as one

of the reasons that led her to undertake her reform. St. Anthony Mary Claret relates the foundation of his Missionaries with the crisis in Christian life that marked the mid-nineteenth century.

At times the Church's greatest need is for a renewal of its life. In these cases, new religious Institutes offer the Church a new, overall view of Christian living, an evangelical life embodied in a form of religious life, whether solitary or cenobitical, monastic, or mendicant. Basil, Benedict, Francis, and Charles de Foucauld all conceived new modes of Christian presence in the world and created new centers of spiritual irradiation.

The relationship of Institutes to a determined historical situation is more readily apparent in the numerous groups that were founded to carry out some interior or exterior ministry: the intercession of contemplatives, evangelization in its various forms, and charitable services. In these cases founders discovered a particular need in the Church and decided to remedy it. That is why, in Institutes of this sort, the chosen ministry appears first in the life of the founder and of his or her first companions. Dominicans, Jesuits, and Claretians were itinerant preachers before they were established as an Institute. Christian educators were already at work in the originating phases of de la Salle's Brothers of the Christian Schools. Many women's Congregations began as pious associations devoted to special activities. The rule of life, structures, and formation of new members all gradually developed around this original axis of ministry. But even in these cases, certain elements of the religious life—celibacy, poverty, community relations—appear from the beginning as essential aspects of the group's dedication to God in the ministry. St. Ignatius, and his companions made promises of chastity and poverty years before they decided to found an Order. St. Anthony Mary Claret and his first Missionaries followed a rule of chastity, poverty, and obedience even before they made any formal commitment and years before their first commitments were replaced by simple vows.

4. The Object of the Founding Inspiration

How can one define the object of the "original inspiration" of these diverse classes of religious families? To what does this inspiration extend? Let us try to ascertain an answer to these questions.

In Institutes founded simply to promote a type of evangelical life, their inspiration necessarily centers on this style of life and on the ways of carrying it out. Members of such groups insist on the fact that the Gospel is the sole reason for their existence in the Church. True as this is, we should be careful not to read any false theological suppositions into the statement. The religious life is not *the* evangelical life, without further ado, as some used to imply in the days when secular life and marriage were regarded more as concessions to human weakness than as genuine Christian vocations. The Gospel is a message for all and contains a rule of life for all. The Gospels themselves expresssly refer to what we now call secular life: Matthew 19: 1-9, on marriage. The life of secular Christians is also an evangelical life, i.e., a life based on the Gospel. Nevertheless, there are a number of deeply valid insights embodied in this way of speaking of the religious life as an evangelical life. In the first place, it stresses what is common to all Christians, rather than their diverse states in life. It affirms that the goal of the religious life (and this is true of matrimony as well) is a life that is faithful to the Gospel. In the second place, it underlines the fact that each of these new religious groups offers the whole Church a clear and fresh witness to the values of the Gospel.

We must say therefore that in the case of the religious Institutes whose aim is to embody a Gospel life in celibacy and community, their "original inspiration" focuses on the quality of life. The Franciscan Rule states exactly that its object is to live "the Holy Gospel, in obedience, without property, and in chastity."[35] But even this is not enough. Why? Because the world view and relative tenor of life are not exactly the same in St. Basil, St. Benedict, St. Francis, or Charles de Foucauld. In each of these cases there is a definite view of community relationships and of the presence of the community in the Church which differs from that of the other groups.

In the more numerous Institutes that were founded for an ecclesial ministry, the "original inspiration" centers on this ministerial relationship with the rest of the Church, and from it the other elements of their spirit and rule of life are derived. But since these groups, too, from their very origins embrace at least some of the elements common to the religious life, the founding inspirations of these Institutes encompasses at one and the same time a reference to their chosen ministry and a call to a particular form of life.

VI

Doctrine

Closely bound up with the vocation of founders is the spiritual doctrine they leave as a legacy to their sons or daughters. We already commented in passing how, in the Middle Ages, the paternity attributed to St. Benedict, or even to the founders of certain famous monasteries, was based on their having bequeathed a rich doctrinal heritage for the nourishment of their followers. This way of understanding paternity in monasticism is reflected in the relationships that existed between the patriarch, St. Benedict, and his monks. Benedict was their *abbas,* their father par excellence. For Benedict, the abbot's mission consisted above all in teaching his monks a life according to the Gospel. In contradistinction to other abbots, St. Benedict still continues teaching this doctrine by way of the Rule professed by numerous monasteries. In fact, the Church has recognized Benedict, in Paul VI's telling phrase, "as an inspired and excellent interpreter of the ways of the Lord."[1]

In a like sense, St. Bonaventure calls his father, St. Francis, "doctor," adding a precise nuance to what he meant: A doctor who first practiced the doctrine which he later proposed in his Rule.[2]

Moreover, we cannot overlook the fact that some founders were extraordinarily enriched with the charism of spiritual teaching. St. Augustine is one of the Fathers of the Church; St. Teresa of Avila and St. Francis de Sales have been canonically recognized as Doctors of the Church; St. Ignatius Loyola has exerted a profound influence of Catholic spirituality.

It is hard to miss the fact that, in the examples referred to above, from St. Benedict to St. Ignatius, the word "doctrine" or "teaching" has been given quite different meanings.

1) In St. Francis of Assisi—and, we would add, St. Basil—there is question of a rule of life. The doctrine involved refers to a concrete, personal, and communitary lifestyle which draws its inspiration from the Gospel.

2) In the case of St. Benedict, too, a rule of life is involved; but in the opening chapters of this Rule, which deal with the art of spirituality, we find a theoretical structuring of this art which has its point of departure in a tradition (Cassian, etc.). There is an exposition of the degrees of humility, for example, and obedience as related to humility.

3) In the case of St. Ignatius Loyola, there seems to be a balance measured out between the doctrine concerning the rule of life for the Society of Jesus and the common spiritual doctrine affecting all Christians: the Constitutions and the Spiritual Exercises.

4) St. Teresa of Avila and St. Francis de Sales also gave their respective daughters a rule of life, but it is obvious that their doctoral mission in the Church, a mission canonically recognized, far transcends the limits of their respective Institutions. Through their spiritual writings both of them reach a far greater audience among the People of God than is reached by the norms they established for their communities.

If the word "doctrine" is taken in the sense of a developed and systematic spiritual theology, then it is obvious that the charism of doctor is not an essential part of the mission of a founder. Not all founders, even great ones like St. Dominic, are Doctors of the Church. We can go further than this: At the beginnings of some great Orders, there is something like a distinction between the charism proper of their father and the doctoral function which one of his illustrious sons assumes. Thus, St. Bernard becomes the Master of Citeaux, which was founded by St. Robert and St. Stephen Harding. St. Bonaventure conceptually organizes the rich experience of St. Francis. St. Thomas Aquinas fixes the theology of the life proper of his Order in the last question of the *Secunda Secundae* of the *Summa Theologica*.

But if the charism of doctor, in this sense, does not form part of the mission of the founder, a certain manner of understanding the religious life as it derives from the ends proper to the Institute does form an indefectible aspect of the original inspiration, and subsequent generations must remain faithful to it. Here we have the core of a theological vision of the religious life. In certain cases this manner of understanding the religious life manifests itself with very original traits, through which new forms of life consecrated to the service of God are created: St. Basil, St. Augustine, St. Dominic, St. Francis of Assisi, St. Ignatius Loyola, St. Angela Merici are all cases in point. From these original traits new theoretical interpretations are derived. Although they coincide in common elements, the theology of Western monasticism is not the theology proper of the Society of Jesus. The theology of St. Teresa of Jesus is quite different from that of St. Angela Merici.

There is yet another important point to consider. The great founders have all enjoyed a distinctive experience of the mystery of Christ, which they have frequently reflected in their writings. Here it is not simply a question of a theology of the religious life, but rather of a spiritual theology in general. Later, some of their disciples have given a theological interpretation to the facts (e.g., St. Bonaventure with respect to St. Francis), and have gone on to develop a spiritual doctrine characteristic of their religious families. This gives rise to a school of spirituality, destined to develop throughout the course of the centuries.

Later on we must come back to this doctrinal aspect of the role of those Christians who were called by God to establish a new religious family. Since some of them were Doctors of the Church or masters of spirituality, or even if they have expressed their own theological point of view and opinions in their writings, especially in their Constitutions, we must ask to what extent all of these doctrinal elements form part of the permanent heritage they left their disciples.

VII

Fullness of Spirit

On two occasions, first in dealing with the greatness of the saints who make up the constellation of founders in the firmament of the Church, and then in reflecting on the legacy of these founders' doctrine, we have remarked on how closely the founding of certain religious Institutes is related to the history of spirituality. At the origins of the various Orders, Congregations, and Societies, we find a person whose holiness has been officially recognized by the Church. The number of processes for the beatification and canonization of founders currently under study is so great that we may reasonably suppose that the list of saint-founders will grow considerably in the coming decades.

1. Sanctity

Many of those who created new religious families in the Church lived the mystery of Christ so strikingly that they had a powerful impact on their contemporaries, even on those who did not know them personally. For example, St. Francis of Assisi died with a tremendous popular reputation for sanctity and was canonized just two years later. St. Anthony Mary Claret was regarded as a popular saint and miracle-worker when he was still a simple itinerant missionary in

Catalonia and the Canary Islands. Others, in contrast, lived quiet lives of dedication to the humble ministries of teaching or charity that they had chosen for themselves and their followers. Nevertheless, their total dedication to the service of God and their neighbor, their charity, their humility, and their prayer life made those who came in contact with them realize their holiness.

First, let us anticipate the possible objection that Orders and Congregations have been a decisive factor in publicizing the virtues of their respective founders. As a general rule, St. Benedict, St. Francis, St. Ignatius, and St. Teresa of Avila are best known by those who have contact with their sons and daughters. This is fully understandable and fitting. It is also true that, in some cases, the sanctity of founders has been used by their Institutes in order to reinforce their unity or raise their own prestige. Later we will talk of the fact that there is a tendency to idealize the founder. Reverence for the founder is an honorable manifestation of love and a filial duty. Of course it can be contaminated by traces of collective pride, which must be purged away, since humility is not only a virtue for the individual religious, but also for the Institute as such. One criterion of authenticity in this matter is catholicity, that is to say that although one feels a special filial love toward one's father or mother, one also feels admiration and devotion toward others. The opposite of this creates a closed and almost sectarian spirit. We personally experienced a case where a preacher from another Institute, called in to deliver a eulogy on our recently canonized founder, could only manage to say that our new Saint owed it all to the Institute to which the preacher belonged!

There have been cases in which the founder's holiness has been invoked in order to reinforce or reinstate the unity of an Institute. Threatened by revolt and schism, the first successors of St. Pachomius insisted on the holiness of their father, in order to give the greater value to the Rule he gave them.

All of this is, or may be, true in certain cases. But even from a merely historical point of view it would be totally unfounded and unjust to attribute a founder's reputation for sanctity to the publicity spread by his or her disciples. Aside from the fact that in many cases this sanctity has been recognized as well-founded by the Church, saints like Augustine, Benedict, Vincent de Paul, Alphonsus Liguori, and Jeanne de Lestonnac had no need for publicity. On the contrary, the spiritual vitality of the frist Franciscans, for example, was largely due to the personal grandeur of the Poor Man of Assisi. The fact that an intense flowering of spirituality is discovered among the first companions of several founders (Benedictines, Franciscans, Jesuits, Claretians, Salesians), is a further confirmation of this opposite fact. Founders managed to radiate a fullness of Christian life. Paul VI said as much in speaking of Don Michele Rua, one of the first disciples of St. John Bosco, during his beatification:

> Don Michele Rua is beatified and glorified today precisely because he was a successor of St. John Bosco, that is to say, his continuator, his son, his disciple and imitator.[1]

The close relationship that exists between the charism of a founder or a foundress and his or her personal holiness is so evident, that Paul VI, in his Apostolic Exhortation *Evangelica Testificatio,* could easily generalize in inviting all religious to be faithful to the example of holiness given them by their founders.[2] And he was fully aware when he said this that he was speaking of a number of Institutes whose fathers and mothers have not yet been canonized. In doing so, the Pope was merely repeating a long-standing tradition. In the seventeenth century, the Venerable Olier described founders as Christians called by God to express the mystery of Christ in a particular way.[3] Two centuries later St. Anthony Mary Claret called them men and women "according to the Heart of God, full of grace and doctrine."[4] Long before both of them St. John of the Cross shared the same opinion. Speaking of the highest mystical graces, the Holy Doctor wrote:

> Few souls arrive at such greatness; but some have, especially those whose virtue and spirit is to be poured out in the succession of their children; God giving such richness and worth to these heads in the first fruits of the spirit, as is in keeping with the greater or lesser following that they are to have in their doctrine and spirit.[5]

There is, then, a close relationship (*proporcion* is the word used by John of the Cross) between the personal holiness of founders and the spirit and doctrine of their sons or daughters. According to the same great Spanish mystic, the highest mystical graces are above all given to those Servants of God who are called to leave many successors in the Church. In this connection he expressly refers to the wounds of St. Francis of Assisi and seems to allude to the transverberation of St. Teresa of Avila.

2. Various Kinds of Gifts

The gifts granted to Holy Founders belong in various categories:

a) Some mystical graces seem to be aimed directly at helping them discover their own personal vocation, out of which that of their Institute will later emerge.

b) In contrast, other graces are granted in order to enlighten and move them toward founding their Orders or Congregations.

These first two classes of mystical or paramystical gifts are related most closely with their charism as founders.

c) Many other divine favors are granted to them for their own personal growth. But even these gifts are in some way connected with their spiritual fruitfulness in the Church.

In the life of the Spirit, as in human biology, personal maturity and the ability to transmit life go hand in hand. It is important to note that St. John of the Cross refers precisely to this third kind of gift when he affirms that the highest of such graces are ordinarily reserved for those whom God calls to create a new religious family. God gives them a deeper and more intense experience of himself, so that others may take advantage of it.

Some founders seem to have had a clear awareness of this exemplaric mission of theirs. St. Francis of Assisi left his followers his *Testament.* Referring to this fact, the first Jesuits prevailed on St. Ignatius Loyola to write his *Autobiography.*[6] St. Teresa of Avila addresses her daughters in her writings. St. Anthony Mary Claret, in obedience to the superior general of his Congregation, composed his autobiography for the formation of his Missionaries.[7] In turn, Claret ordered his spiritual daughter, Saint Micaela of the Blessed Sacrament, to write an account of her life and of the graces she had received, since the spiritual gifts with which she had been enriched belonged in some way to her daughters whom she had a duty to confirm in their vocation.[8]

Through which channels do these graces of founders reach their sons and daughters? At the deepest level there is only one: the Holy Spirit, who builds up the Christian community through the gifts given to each of its members. But founders play an active role, albeit instrumental, in this process of transmission:

a) Above all, they intercede for their Institutes through their prayers, their sufferings, and their very lives. Autobiographies, diaries, and letters show the extent to which their works figure in the relationships between founders and God;

b) Second, founders seem to have enjoyed a special power of persuasion. They were more or less extraordinary personalities, and the eyes and ears of their followers seem to have been attuned to pick up their exhortations and example.

Mother Angela Truszkowska, foundress of the Sisters of St. Felix of Cantalice, in a letter to her spiritual director confesses:

> When it's a question of myself, I don't know how to disentangle myself, I can't distinguish what's good from what's bad. But when it comes to others, that's a different case. There isn't anyone, so to speak, who doesn't receive my influence, when I want them to. Without doubt, this is a gift that isn't for myself, but for others.[9]

This process goes on, even after the founder's death. The *Life of Anthony* by St. Athanasius, the *Life of Augustine* by Possidius, the first biographies of St. Francis, the *Life of Ignatius* by Ribadaneyra, and the *Life of Archbishop Claret* by Father Clotet were all composed with a clear intent of presenting a model to their respective disciples. Frequently the oldest documents, biographies, memoirs, or simple notes on founders, were drafted by those who had known them personally. These writings therefore manifest the deep imprint that these Servants of God left on those who surrounded them.

3. Idealization

But we have already noted that the first generations tend to paint a larger than life image of their founders. All we have to do is to compare the successive buildup of this image in the witnesses, even when founders appear in the earliest days as surrounded by a living halo. What happens is that founders are soon transformed into symbols of the ideals of the group they founded, thanks to the process of idealization we have already referred to. The history of the origins of a religious family fulfills in this respect a role similar to that which myths of origin play in various primitive and not-so-primitive societies. The earliest days of an Institute are generally referred to in the way that the French Revolution of 1789 is referred to in the Republic of France, or as the "Founding Fathers" are referred to in the United States, or as the Soviet Revolution is referred to in socialist countries, not to mention the "Golden Age" in antiquity. This is quite understandable since it answers a deeply felt human need. Human groups tend to express their ideals, and hence their collective identity, much more effectively through idealized models than through doctrinal formulations. In the ancient *Lives of the Fathers,* and later in the legends concerning St. Francis of Assisi, the earliest days of the monachate or the Franciscan movement are represented as a sort of paradise regained. In the successive lives of St. Pachomius, the process of idealization and canonization is quite visible. The most ancient of these lives tells us of a fault of impatience with his brother incurred by Pachomius while he was building the first dwelling for his future disciples. Later there is an attempt to attribute the fault to Pachomius' brother, even though this deprives the narrative of logical sequence.[10]

But we must not confuse this process of idealization with a process of falsification. In idealization real traits are made use of, even though they are sometimes taken out of historical, personal, or social context. Ordinarily, for example, there is a reluctance to speak of the human limitations of the founder. Nevertheless, it is beautiful to see how grace keeps overcoming these human limitations and opening up through them. Still, the traits that are emphasized are real. The oldest documents tend to paint a splendid image of the father or mother, even when certain traits are not developed or before any legends have taken final shape. Yet even in these cases we must bear in mind that the legends that are forming around Pachomius, Benedict, Francis, Peter of Nolasco, and the Seven Founders of the Servites are all in some degree historical in that they demonstrate the profound influence these persons exercised on their first disciples. Legends do not develop around unimportant persons. At the same time, these legends frequently underline some of the typical traits of the founder. It may well be that St. Francis was not born in a stable, but such a story says a good deal about the Saint's likeness to Christ.

4. Sanctity and Human Shortcomings

The fact of the holiness of founders and foundresses is evident in a great number of cases, as we have seen. Does this mean that it is enough for a Christian, from the mere fact that he or she has left behind a community or evangelical movement, to be considered a person of proven holiness? The exemplary virtue of many founders and foundresses has been recognized by the Church, and a great number of Causes of Beatification that are presently being discussed involve men or women Servants of God who started religious Institutes.

Nevertheless, the fact of their sanctity cannot be automatically taken for granted. The Spirit of God, whose freedom and power are absolute, does not need human virtue in order to carry out a great work. Indeed, God frequently chooses weak instruments. Again, the elements of human frailty and fallibility must always be reckoned with. The Christian who is called by God to establish a religious family is capable of not responding to a grace that is given not for him or her alone, but also for others. And this capability remains even after he or she has received the original inspiriation, or has already begun to put it into execution.

Hence it is that the Christian called by God to this work cannot but feel an acute sense of responsibility. A passage in *Mutuae Relationes* adverts to this:

> The specific charismatic note of any Institute demands both of the founder and of his disciples a continual examination regarding fidelity to the Lord: docility to his Spirit, intelligent attention to circumstances, and an outlook cautiously directed toward the signs of the times.[11]

This is exactly what the decree *Perfectae Caritatis* requires of religious Institutes: a return to the Gospel and to the founder (under-standing that the latter is already dead) and attention to the present. This is required of both founders and foundresses, and of their disciples, doubtless because of an awareness of the many present founders who are still alive, and of the numerous founders who will come in the future.

VIII

Charism and Institution

Thus far we have focused our attention on the birth and development of the charism in a man or woman Servant of God, whereby a religious family comes into existence among the People of God. This charism, like all charisms, is ultimately aimed toward the well-being of the ecclesial community. In fact, as we have written elsewhere,[1] the birth of the various forms of religious life and of the various Institutes are absolutely incomprehensible if we do not bear in mind that they are varied responses of the Holy Spirit to the different needs of the Church, especially those needs that are most sensibly felt during the period in which these Institutes appear. Religious life itself in general has, insofar as it is a life, a ministerial sense.[2]

But when these charisms erupt at the surface, from the interior where the Spirit of Pentecost is burning like lava, they must necessarily push against the hard crust which has been hardening for centuries. The People of God are not just a charismatic reality (although they are a charismatic reality essentially), but also an institutional entity. The Church has its firm structures and its ministers, people whom God certainly helps in their care for his people, but people who are likewise conditioned by a certain mentality. They derive this mentality and this conditioning from their time, their national authority, and are burdened with serious responsibilities.

Indeed, the relationship between founding charism and institution is not restricted to inherent tensions with the Church-as-institution, since a founding charism will itself give rise to its own particular institution. This is inevitable and indispensable for its survival. The initial group, frequently loose, free, and prophetic (the first Franciscans and the first itinerant Jesuits) end up institutionalizing themselves by creating structures of government and apostolate and by framing norms for their security. What would be left today of the charisms of Francis, Teresa, or Ignatius if it were not for their respective institutions? Are they not the very ones who keep the memory of their founders alive for successive generations? Certainly, however, institutionalization also creates problems.

For the moment let us fix our attention on the difficulties that can arise when the creative charism meets the established structures of the Church. Vatican II in its constitution *Lumen Gentium* has left us a few words on the encounter between founders and foundresses, on the one hand, and the ecclesiastical hierarchy, on the other:

> The hierarchy, following with docility the prompting of the Holy Spirit, accepts the rules presented by outstanding men and women and authentically approves these rules after further adjustments. It also aids by its vigilant and safeguarding authority those Institutes variously established for the building up of Christ's Body in order that these same Institutes may grow and flourish according to the Spirit of the founders.[3]

We have already referred in passing to the fact that the Council defines the attitude of shepherds towards these "outstanding men and women" in much the same way that it had previously described the role of those who preside over charisms in the Church.[4] History shows that this has ordinarily been the case. St. Athanasius, a bishop, encounters the novelty of eremitic monasticism and interprets it for the whole Church by way of his *Life of Anthony.* The spontaneous groups created by Macrina and Basil move ahead cautiously, especially after the condemnation suffered by Eustace of Sebaste, but even so they end up imposing themselves on the Church of Asia Minor. Gregory the Great would eventually come to speak almost fulsomely of Benedict, his sanctity and his Rule. One of the most surprising things is the esteem in which Francis of Assisi and Dominic de Guzman were held by popes who by all means upheld an image of the Church (as a political power in the feudal system) that was diametrically opposed to the Church of the Poor which these Saints championed. Ignatius Loyola obtained papal approval for his Society despite all the suspicions that its innovations provoked among traditional circles. In all of these cases we find it hard to doubt that the Spirit who stood behind these founders was also standing behind these shepherds, and that the latter allowed themselves to be led in great docility by the divine Spirit.

Nevertheless, these words of Vatican II can by no means be understood as expressing a universal historical law. If we try to apply them to all cases we must understand them as "what ought to be," rather than "what has always been the case." For there are notable cases in which the hierarchy has opposed founders and foundresses, sometimes occasioning great sufferings for them, sometimes limiting or changing the direction that they had marked out. We will say something more on this subject in the following chapter where we treat of the sufferings of these "outstanding men and women." For the moment we need only recall the way in which the Roman Curia rejected the ideas of Mary Ward and only approved her Institute three centuries later. The Order of the Visitation, as originally envisioned by Jeanne Fremyot de Chantal and Francis de Sales, was radically changed by the hierarchy. Angela Merici wanted the prototype of the Ursulines to be a sort of Secular Institute without habit but, after Charles Borromeo changed them into a religious Congregation, the French hierarchy ended up changing them into an Order with solemn vows and cloister. Apostolic Congregations of women had to move with a great deal of caution for a considerable period: In fact, official theology would not bring itself to refer to their apostolates as ministries until our own day. And we may add that Institutes of simple vows were not recognized as Institutes of the religious life, in the strict sense, until the end of the nineteenth century and practically until the promulgation of the Code of Canon Law. No doubt about it: It costs churchmen, shepherds, theologians, and canonists a great deal to follow the creative movements of the Holy Spirit. God always seems to run ahead of us.

The document we have quoted above, *Mutuae Relationes,* has recognized both these facts:

Every authentic charism implies certain elements of genuine originality and of special initiative for the spiritual life of the Church. In its surroundings it may even cause difficulties, since it is not always and immediately easy to recognize it as coming from the Spirit.[5]

The text doesn't tell us exactly which person or persons will find it hard to distinguish the pneumatic origin of these innovative elements, but it is fairly clear that it must refer mainly to those who are officially called to the discernment of spirits. If the founder or foundress is called upon to maintain communion with the Church despite all, the words of *Lumen Gentium,* pointing to the role which bishops are called upon to exercise regarding charisms, presuppose among bishops a great responsibility in the sometimes difficult task of acknowledging them.

IX

The Sufferings of Founders and Foundresses

Paging through the lives of founders and foundresses we are struck by another fact: the great frequency with which these men and women were subject to severe trials. We do not just mean the difficulties they had to overcome initially in order to pursue their vocation, nor the efforts it cost some of them to define the fundamental traits of the spirit that was to animate their works (e.g., the long process of discernment St. Ignatius had to go through before defining the kind of poverty professed in the Society of Jesus).

Rather, we mean the harsh opposition raised against them, even by their own disciples. This is an interesting, sorrowful, but at the same time glorious aspect of the history of not a few foundations.

In some cases founders have had to face the rise of certain tendencies among their first disciples which they knew to be contrary to their spirit. Even in cases where there was no direct opposition to the founder, there was an effort to lead the Institute along a different path. We can see this in the lives of St. Pachomius and St. Francis of Assisi.

In the Pachomian Congregation (Egypt, fourth century) there seems to have been a strong tendency, influenced by the earlier eremitical monachate, which stressed rigorism and mortification rather than communion. Pachomius was obliged to remove Theodore, a holy man but one of an entirely different spirit, from the post of assistant, and as Pachomius lay dying he entrusted the government of his Institute to another. Shortly afterwards, one part of the Institute rose up in protest, and Orsisius, the superior, was obliged to appoint Theodore as his assistant.[1]

Centuries later St. Francis of Assisi had to struggle painfully with the difficulties that his new rule gave rise to among those of his brethren who were not sufficiently well identified with his spirit: those who wandered through the streets without due obedience, the new poverty movements that had become alienated from the Church, the desire of some of his ministers to adopt a more traditional rule of life. All of these things embittered the last years of the Saint's life, to the point that he was obliged to appoint a minister general for the Order and have recourse to the Roman Curia in order to clear up the situation.[2] We can imagine what this meant for Francis: perplexities, sufferings, long prayer, second thoughts.

In other cases the Institutes were embroiled in jurisdictional struggles between popes and kings. St. Alphonsus Liguori had to witness the division of his Congregation—by no less than the Pope!—into two diverse organizational units and had to watch and accept the fact that the Pope appointed another superior general for the houses located in the Papal States.[3] Sometimes an Institute was divided by bishops, each of whom claimed jurisdiction over it. The author of this study has researched a very sad case of a Spanish foundation, the Missionary Sisters of the Immaculate Conception, founded by Mother Alphonse Cavin. The sisters were divided into two groups by the bishops of Barcelona and Tarragona, and the foundress was deposed.[4]

At other times the struggle was waged directly against the person of the founder, although the Institute itself always has had to pay the consequences. The most famous case of this sort is that of St. Joseph Calasanz, the founder of the Piarists, who was slandered in accusations to the Roman Curia. The Saint was deposed by Urban VIII, judged by the Holy Office, and saw his Institute reduced to a simple federation of autonomous houses by Innocent X.[5]

Equally well known are the trials through which St. Teresa of Jesus and St. John of the Cross had to pass in order to be able to proceed with their reform of the Carmelite Order. St. John was first kidnapped and rudely incarcerated by his own coreligionists; then, years later, he was prevented from holding any governing office in the

Order. Another long and lamentable chapter could be written on the oppression and persecution which women have had to suffer, owing to the prejudicial assumption that they were unable to govern by themselves. Perhaps the most famous case in this connection is that of Mary Ward (1586-1644), the great English lady who founded the Institute of the Blessed Virgin Mary. She had received the inspiration to found an apostolic Institute for women with a centralized government, like those already formed by men's Institutes. This whole idea seemed scandalous to certain English clergy, and they attacked it publicly. The storm of controversy was carried to Rome where Mary valiantly defended her cause, but in vain: Her Institute was abolished by the Propaganda Fide. Looked upon as a rebel, she spent a period of incarceration in Munich and at length returned to England where she died without having been able to carry out her project.[6]

More commonly a foundress had to deal with a priest assigned by the bishop as ecclesiastical superior to govern the Institute. One result of this system was that the Institute had to put up with a number of vexing and discriminatory measures imposed by the diocesan chancery. On a number of occasions, because of the interference or indifference of these ecclesiastical superiors, one part of the community would rise up against the foundress. Maria Teresa Gerhardinger (1797-1874), the foundress of the School Sisters of Notre Dame, could only look on as the Archbishop of Munich, who was still opposed to centralized government for women's Institutes, divided her Congregation into simple autonomous houses, subject to diocesan chanceries.[7] Mary Clara Pfaender (1827-1882), the foundress of the Franciscan Sisters of Salzkotten (Wheaton, Illinois), had to suffer still more. The vicar general had her deposed, and the foundress spent the last years of her life exiled in Rome, in dire poverty. She died alone, assisted only by a sister who had agreed to accompany her in exile.[8] Bonifacia Rodriguez, the foundress of the Sister Servants of Saint Joseph in Spain, and Maria Rosa Zangara, the foundress of the Daughters of Mercy and of the Cross in Sicily, were both practically alienated from their Institutes and spent the last years of their lives confined to a house of their communities and kept incommunicado from the rest of their sisters. The number of foundresses deposed from the government of their Institutes is as sad as it is impressive: St. Jeanne de Lestonnac (+1640), Blessed Alix Le Clerq

(+1622), Mother Alphonse Cavin (+1868), St. Rafaela of the Sacred Heart, besides those already mentioned: Mary Ward, Theresa Gerhardinger, Clara Pfaender, Bonifacia Rodriguez, and Mary Rosa Zangara. In a more limited sense, Mother Antonia Paris, the foundress of the Claretian Missionary Sisters, had to suffer considerably because a bishop obliged her sisters living in his diocese to refuse to acknowledge her as their superior.

The sufferings of not a few founders and foundresses, often because of the meddling of ministers of the Church, is a historical fact which leaves a painful impression on us all. It would be wrong for us to deny it, although we must not exaggerate it. The great majority of founders and foundresses died surrounded by the esteem of all and the love of their sons or daughters. But even the sufferings that had befallen a minority of these outstanding men and women are enough to give rise to a number of searching questions. We believe that this matter has been addressed for the first time in a recent document of the Holy See. The document in question is *Mutuae Relationes,* issued jointly by the Congregation of Bishops and the Congregation of Religious and Secular Institutes on May 14, 1978:

> The true relation between genuine charism, with its perspective of genuineness and interior suffering, carries with it an unvarying history of the connection between charism and cross which, above every motive that may justify misunderstandings, is supremely helpful in discerning the authenticity of a vocation.[9]

According to this text there is a deep relationship between charism and cross. We must reflect on this relationship, although we believe that it is also illuminating to reflect first of all on the human causes of these sufferings. Even at the risk of generalizing, we can detect one principal motive: the shock between the creative newness of charism and the entrenchment of institution, whose representatives are conditioned by a certain mentality and frequently strive to defend their alleged rights. Since we have already dealt with the relationships between charism and institution, we would not like to repeat ourselves here.

But it would be superficial and simplistic to reduce the idea of the sufferings of founders and foundresses to the clash between the creative newness of their charisms and the conservative mentality of those who represent and govern the institution. Indeed, there are numerous cases where the acute sufferings of founders were not caused by this sort of clash. For example, we have already cited the case of Alphonsus Liguori, who was caught up as an innocent by-stander in a struggle between the king and the papacy which caused him deep moral sufferings that would haunt and trouble him inwardly until his dying day. There are occasions, too, where the father or mother has been rejected by the very community he or she founded. In this connection, how could we forget the sufferings and isolation of John of the Cross, the first member of the reform of the male branch of the Carmelites. At other times the greatest sufferings did not come from the outside, but from the inner depths of the founders themselves. Paul of the Cross, the founder of the Passionists, underwent one of the most terrible nights of the spirit on historical record. He did, of course, suffer from exterior causes, such as misunderstandings of the Curia relating to his various attempts to gain the approval of his Institute and had to undergo internal crises of the Institute with his brothers. But above all he suffered interior desolation, a sense of spiritual abandonment and fierce temptations throughout many long years.[10]

The sufferings brought on founders by their own Institutes often seem to have a particular meaning for them. These trials appear frequently in their lives as part of a deep purification, a particular form of the dark night of the spirit, during which God purifies the legitimate love which these Saints and Servants of God have for their works, from the least roots of human attachment. These great persons are human beings, after all, and it is not surprising to suggest that their maternal or paternal love may be mixed with a certain human satisfaction in their work or a certain attachment to those involved in it. The aim of the night of the spirit is to purify them from these last traces of self-love. The most effective means for bringing about this purification is the Institute itself, which is in one way or another transformed into a cross for the founder or foundress. In some saints the night of the spirit may arise from some other quarter, but the effect is the same.

Still, the personal purification of the founders or foundresses does not seem to exhaust the depths of meaning involved in these trials.

We must also take into account the co-redeeming value of their sufferings. The founding charism which they have received is a source of life and the giving of life in the Spirit, within the living context of Jesus, is always related to the Cross. These sufferings are, then, part of the intercession before God on behalf of their sons or daughters, which is proper to founders and foundresses.

X

From Founder to Group:
The Community Charism

Having analyzed various data that commonly appear in the lives of founders and foundresses, we must now investigate which of their aspects are passed on to their families and must therefore be regarded as constitutive elements of the community charism. Referring to founders' charisms and their transmission to the Institutes created by them, Paul VI used two different expressions. Speaking to the Benedictines of Subiaco, he told them that they were "guided by the charism" of the patriarch of Western monasticism. He was not speaking here of the transmission of the charism, but was stating that the religious family should be inspired by the personal charism of its father.[1] In contrast, speaking to the Passionist sisters a few weeks later, he told them that "they had made their own" the charism of St. Paul of the Cross.[2] Finally, he told the Congregation of St. Joseph of Murialdo that they were "heirs of the charism" of their founder.[3] These are two aspects of the same reality: religious, in order to discover their community charism and be faithful to it, must draw their inspiration from the personal charism of their founder. It may also be said with the Pope, that the charism passes from father or mother to their sons and daughters.

1. Aspects of the Founder that do *Not* Pass on to the Institute

In the transmission of charism from the founder to the Order or Congregation, all that is strictly personal to the founder cannot be included. We will list some aspects that must be excluded.

First we must exclude the sufferings of many founders. Certainly, through these trials, the Saints and Servants of God brought down many divine graces on their descendants. Paternity and maternity always entail suffering. In the Mystical Body these sufferings are a source of spiritual fecundity. But a call to suffering is ordinarily a personal vocation, not a community one. An Institute is not founded to suffer more for the Church. The Lord distributes trials directly. However, what can be part of a group's vocation is the spirit of self-sacrifice and reparation or a particular communion with the Passion of Christ. In this case, the founder's sufferings can have an exemplary value and can serve as the prototypical realization of the common vocation of the group. For example, the harsh night of the spirit through which St. Paul of the Cross passed, although it was in itself something strictly personal, can nevertheless show to what extent a Passionist should be disposed to go in realizing that association with the Passion of the Lord that is part of the spirit of the Institute. The Pope was alluding precisely to this in the discourse to the Passionists mentioned above.

Second, we must exclude from the charism the *degree of sanctity* reached by the founder. The degree of communion with Christ and the graces related with it are something strictly personal and as such nontransferable. Nevertheless, we must repeat here what we said concerning sufferings. This sanctity has been a rich source of graces for the group, since greater closeness to Christ bestows a greater intercessory power. Moreover, this sanctity is also a permanent source of inspiration for successive generations. Still more, the founder and foundress have lived the Christian life with certain more or less outstanding personal characteristics, characteristics which correspond to his or her own vocation, as well as to that of his or her sons and daughters. This particular experience of the mystery of Christ may give rise to a school of spirituality or at least to a certain spiritual ambience. These form part of the tradition of the Institute.

Third, the charism of *doctor* with which some founders were graced is something strictly personal and is not passed on to their Institutes. Nevertheless, some founders, or rather their disciples, in interpreting the experience of their founder, have created a doctrinal school of spirituality which, insofar as it is a doctrinal formulation, does not pertain to the charism but is more or less closely bound up with it and hence belongs to the living tradition of the Institute. It is natural for sons and daughters to continue the work of their fathers or mothers, or that of their first interpreters. This does not mean, however, that every religious is obliged to follow the opinions of their founder-doctor to the letter. A school is a living tradition which is continually being completed, enriched, and reinterpreted.

But founders and foundresses—all of them—have a particular way of seeing the religious life, a way related to the ends which moved them to found their Institutes. The way in which Clare of Assisi, Louise de Marillac, and Teresa of Jesus interpret the religious life is closely related to the charism of their religious families. This fact shines through in an extraordinarily strong way in certain founders or inspirers of Institutes: Augustine, Benedict, Francis, Ignatius, and Anthony Claret. In these cases this new or renewed way of religious living is closely related with charism: It is an integral part of the original explanation of the charism given by the founders themselves.

But this charism-related phenomenon does not extend to everything that they thought or wrote themes on concerning the religious life. The particular form of life which they developed is one thing, while the different doctrinal colorations they attribute to certain aspects of this life is quite another. Frequently they only repeated a determined view that was common in their milieu or simply echoed certain arguable theological opinions. We know, for example, that for many centuries, from the time of the Fathers to the beginning of the twelfth century, the dominant point of view regarded the monachate as a full form of Christian life (and this is to some extent beyond discussion). But this was also joined to another way of thinking that looked on the married laity as persons who were not strong enough to follow the way of the perfect. This was the famous theory of the two ways, one for strong adults, the other for weak children, a theory which we cannot accept today. Yet this theory stands behind a good number of monastic texts, even though St. Benedict, whose fine sense corrects the *Rule of the Master,* does not express it. Certain founders have given reasons for practicing obedience that we have a hard time accepting. It was held, for example, that obedience does not arise from the fact that we have committed ourselves to search in common for the saving will of God and that this will is proposed to us by legitimate authority, so that we in turn may sacrifice our own wills in the interest of communion. Rather, following an inverse perspective, it was held that the superior was established so that we should not follow our wills and so that we should mortify ourselves, as if this were the primary value in obedience. The Master of the anonymous Rule dating from the beginning of the sixth century thought along these lines, and a number of later thinkers echoed his thought. Between the seventeenth and nineteenth centuries, a strictly disciplinary, quasi-collegial image of community life and of the superior was accepted. This image is reflected in a number of texts by founders. None of this is of permanent value. A serious and honest study of such texts is needed in order to determine which elements are passé and which of them have permanent value, either in themselves or because of their relationship with the charism.

2. Community Charism

Turning now to the positive study of what personality traits of the founder are transformed into a group charism, we must recall that in essence the charism is that vocation, common to all in the Institute, which the founder or foundress first discovered for himself or herself. In other words, the charism of a religious family coincides with the object of the inspiration which was granted to the one who gave it its being in the Church. In this we are being faithful to the fundamental meaning of the word "charism" as used in the New Testament: a gift of the Spirit given to someone for the good of the Church. More commonly put, it is a gift which defines one's vocation in the People of God, both on the level of lifestyle (1 Cor. 7:7) and of ecclesial ministries. Speaking of a group charism, we go beyond the New

Testament, which always speaks of a gift given to a person or really to persons, although not as forming a particular group. But although we go beyond the New Testament in applying it, we do not go against its doctrine.

We must note that charism and vocation are always given by the Holy Spirit directly to a person. It is the Risen Lord, through the movements and lights of his Spirit, who distributes charisms and calls people to diverse states of life and ministries in his Body. No one beneath him can appropriate any authority over charisms and vocations. Vatican II tells us that it is the concern of the hierarchy to discern them and regulate their exercise. But to discern them is not at all to bestow them.

We enter a religious Institute because we realize that our vocation essentially coincides with that of its members and with the aims which this institution pursues. Moreover, we stay with a religious Institute because we are attracted by the spiritual figure of its founder, even though we may discover this at a later moment. In effect, what we do is to advert to the likeness between our own gifts that orient us toward a mission in the Church and those gifts received by the one who gave life to this Institute. This is true even in the first generation of disciples or companions of the founder. The first followers get together with the founder because they share in his or her personal call. And this personal vocation implies determined graces which dispose them to fulfill this mission in the Church. Later, when the group begins to be established and institutionalized, the charism is described in the Rule, Constitutions, or Statutes.

Father Nadal stated that the particular graces of each religious family are given to them through the founder. We need not imagine this as some sort of mediation in the strict sense. This is what happens: 1) The founder is the first to receive the vocation and then the first followers receive it, either by having it proposed to them by the founder or by seeing it realized in him or her. It is by all means the Lord who gives founders these sons or daughters: "After the Lord gave me Friars," as St. Francis of Assisi describes it in his *Testament*.[4] 2) As for the graces in the vocation, they are implicit in it, but we must recognize a certain power of intercession in the Saint or Servant of God in whom this vocation first flowers.

3. Is the Charism Transmitted?

From what we have said it can be clearly understood whether one may rightly speak of the transmission of the charism when the word "charism" is used in the proper sense. Today, in fact, writers and speakers refer rather frequently to the charism transmitted through founders to their disciples. The Vatican document *Mutuae Relationes* does so when it speaks of founders' charisms "as an experience of the Spirit transmitted to their disciples to be lived."[5] The charism, as we have said, always comes directly from the Lord. It is not given by the Church, by any member of the Church (including founders and foundresses), or by the religious community. The Lord, by means of his Spirit, gives it to each individual: It is the vocation to a form of *sequela* or following of Christ, or to an ecclesial ministry and by that very fact to a certain type of spirituality, together with the grace which makes a Christian capable of following that life, developing that ministry and living that spirituality. Individuals enter a community because they discover a certain identity (never a total one) between their personal gift and the gift received through the founder or foundress and their other sons or daughters.

And yet something is transmitted which is very much related to the charism, and therefore in a broad sense one may speak of the transmission of the charism. The gift received by the father or mother, and directly from God by their followers, is collectively cultivated, proposed in spiritual doctrine to new generations, deepened, and actualized. Its principal elements, the aim of the Institute or the "primordial concern" of the community, are described in the Constitutions, the form of life and spiritual environment are also described in them, as a point of confrontation and source of light and nourishment for successive generations. In this less proper sense, the charism is transmitted.

4. Elements of the Community Charism

Bearing all of this in mind, we can now proceed to enumerate the constitutive elements of the charism which a religious family has in common with the man or woman who gave them their existence:

1) In the case of a call to the religious life, the charism consists above all in a vocation to a type of Christian existence consecrated to the service of God through celibacy and common life. Since this tenor of life is a profession in the Church, a certain way of relating to the rest of the People of God is an integral part of the charism.

2) In Institutes created with a specific aim (contemplative intercessory prayer or some external activity), this ministry is not only part of the charism, but the specific element around which this charism has developed toward its fullness. The concrete mode of living and religious life cannot be understood without explicit, constant reference to its proper ministry.

3) A certain spirituality, rooted in the common elements of the religious life and in the elements proper to a concrete way of life, is a natural consequence of this vocation. Vocation is in fact the dynamic source of every spirituality.

4) In those cases where the founder enjoyed a particular experience of the mystery of Christ from which a spiritual doctrine has developed, then this way of living the life of the Spirit also forms part of the community charism. Although the stigmata of St. Francis, the transfixing of St. Teresa, and the eucharistic grace of St. Anthony Mary Claret were personal, nontransferable gifts, the way in which those Saints related to God, the aspects of the life of Christ that most attracted them, their way of living ecclesial communion, all have an exemplary value for their sons and daughters. There is a way of looking at life that is characteristically Benedictine, Franciscan, Jesuit, a way that is proper to Carmelite nuns, Visitandines, or Sisters of Perpetual Adoration.

XI

Communitary Charism and the Personalities of the Founders and Foundresses

After what we have said it might seem that the question of the relationships between founders and foundresses and the charism of their religious families has been sufficiently clarified. But things are not as simple as they might appear at first sight. For even in the manner in which founders lived the vocation they have in common with their followers they acted as concrete individuals. We must never forget that divine grace is always given to real living persons with their own individual temperament and qualities, yet formed through a series of experiences and conditioned by the environment in which they lived. Not only the temperament and character of a person, but also time and society have a deep influence on the religious experience of the saints.

Founders also respond to the divine call according to the inward tendencies of their psyches and are immersed in their own time and society. St. Maria Micaela of the Blessed Sacrament and St. Joaquina de Vedruna evoke a particular epoch in the Spanish Church, just as Mother Seton and Mother Cabrini do in the American Church. St. Jane Frances de Chantal was as typical a French lady as her niece, Mme. de Sevigne, was somewhat later. The Greek sensibility of St. Basil is manifest in the way he views community life. St. Francis of

Assisi holds an important place in Italian literature, as St. Teresa of Avila does in Spanish literature. The examples could go on for pages, but the few we have mentioned suffice to show the extent to which founders are real, living, human beings. Their being conditioned by the time and the society in which they grew up does not limit the universality of their message. A classic author in literature or philosophy is not one who escapes his or her time (that would be impossible), but one who manages to express permanent values by way of the concrete situations of that time. The same happens in the history of the religious life.

1. The Nationality of the Founder

The question of the relationship between community charism and the nationality of the first members of an Institute has taken several forms. In theory there is nothing against a religious institution being limited to certain geographical zones. East and West have had distinctive forms of manasticism, following diverse traditions. But in the West, since the thirteenth century, religious Institutes have generally taken the form of centrally organized institutions: In these national frontiers have no value. Members of many different nationalities live together in the same family and share the same vocation and spirit. Some Orders, such as the Dominicans and Jesuits, were international groups from the outset. Others, such as the Franciscans, spread rapidly through different countries. However, most Institutes developed slowly and only later came to cross the borders of their country or origin.

In this latter case the institution may have set its roots so deeply in the society of the mother country that the universality of its message suffers. As new generations from other countries enter, they may undergo a certain culture shock at what they consider to be a foreign mentality. This is followed by a reaction against the French, Spanish, or Italian elements in the Institute or, in the case of America, against the European. This has been the main reason why a number of Congregations, especially those of women, have decided to separate and form a new group. This can definitely be a form of enrichment for the Church, although the original group may lose vitality. Other groups maintain their unity, but undergo a series of crises until a fuller formulation of their aims and spirit can be developed. Clearly, the "national" as such does not pertain to the charism, although the founder may only have been able to actualize it within the context of his or her own national heritage.

2. The Time of the Founder

It is more difficult and delicate to resolve the question of how charism relates to a certain period in the history of the Church. Often the profile of religious families has been profoundly shaped by the period in which they had their greatest development and growth. Benedictine monasticism evokes a patristic and medieval vision of the world and the Church. The Franciscan movement can be adequately understood only if we take into account the historical and social situation in which it was born. Clerical Institutes have a close relationship with the Church's self-understanding in the light of Trent. The problem is more acute where an Institute has come to be the prototype of religious life and the most active center of spirituality in a determined period. Not only its spirituality, but its structures of life and government may appear to be the result of its temporal setting.

This question is all the more pressing today, since it seems that we find ourselves in the dawn of a new stage in the history of spirituality. The first glimmerings of this age appeared in the mid-nineteenth century, grew brighter during the first half of the twentieth century with the biblical and liturgical movements, as well as those of the lay apostolate and the renewal of spiritual theology, and burst upon the whole Church with Vatican II. This spirituality is biblical, sacramental, liturgical, and strongly community-oriented. In the United States it has also taken a decidedly mystical and charismatic turn. While monastic communities, because of these aspects we have just mentioned, find themselves once more in their element, apostolic communities founded between Trent and the beginning of the twentieth century have had to adapt and renew. Moreover, the heightened sensibility of our times to the rights of the individual person and the growth of democracy have presented a challenge to certain forms of religious government.

It seems clear that religious Institutes were never established in order to perpetuate a determined period in the history of the Church. Time is never a constitutive element of a charism. If we agree that monasticism is the form of religious life that corresponds to the world view proper to the Fathers of the Church, we might well conclude that the spiritual synthesis common to the patristic era is proper to monasticism. Why, then, should we exclude the fact that certain tendencies in spirituality that developed in the West out of the *devotio moderna* (a special way of understanding the relationship between person and community, a special recognition in favor of mental prayer) might be permanent traits characterizing groups that have appeared after Trent? The answer given to this question depends on whether or not one accepts a number of criteria:

1) Do these traits have a permanent value, or are we dealing here only with episodic facts? For example, a narrow and rigidly methodical way of understanding mental prayer, as well as a predominantly disciplinary concept of community life, both of which were quite widespread in the nineteenth century, have fallen out of favor and no one should lament their almost total disappearance. In the patristic period and in the Middle Ages, there were commonly held points of view that can no longer be maintained today.

2) Are these spiritual traits related to the vocation of an Institute in the Church? In our opinion, the greater importance given mental prayer or certain forms of interrelationship in community, in apostolic Institutes, are a consequence of their apostolic vocation and not just the product of a particular social setting. Hence, these Institutes may correct certain points of view and enrich their life with contributions from the liturgical movement, but they should by no means strive to convert themselves into monastic institutions.

The problem of the permanent value of a certain system of government has emerged with greater insistency in our days, since there is often a great difference between the socio-political environment in which we live and that in which many founders lived, and because our sense of communal values is often quite changed. Those who follow a tradition in which communion is the predominant trend and in which the horizontal dimension of community is stressed, may feel more at home today, whereas those Institutes which stress a vertical line of government feel obliged to defend themselves from environmental pressures. Let us limit our discussion to the facts. There are those, both within and without the Benedictine Order, who have viewed the institution of the abbot as a reflection of family or political structures in the time of Benedict. Father Adalbert de Vogüé, in his well-known study of the abbot and the monastery, affirmed the precedence of the abbot and stated his resistance to the notion of any socio-political influence on the institution of the abbot.[1] But later, in the prologue to the English version of his study, he notes his awareness of running counter to community tendencies today, and insinuates that it is possible to situate the abbot in this newer context.[2] The problem is a real one: A document which reflects the conclusions of a meeting of abbots and monks in 1968 spoke of the political contamination of the image of the abbot and the time of the re-establishment of the monachate in Europe, after the breakdown caused by the French Revolution.[3]

Passing on to the modern apostolic Institutes, not a few of them, even while maintaining a centralized vertical structure, have introduced, especially on the level of the local community, a dynamic of consensus and a sensibility of communion. A number of women's apostolic communities have introduced deep changes in their governments, limiting the field of the executive and providing several mechanisms for community participation in the decision-making process. In contrast, a highly authorized representative of the Society of Jesus, in a meeting of Superiors General, went against a major current at the meeting and stated that government by consensus or by majority decision was not possible in their Institute. It is evident that the structures of government have a close relationship with the identity of some Institutes, while they do not in orders.

3. The Founder as an Individual

The problem of relationships between the individual personality of the man or woman founder and their founding charism can be viewed on different levels. In some cases the problem can be resolved rather easily; in others, it is more difficult and delicate to formulate a response. No one questions the fact that these men and women Servants of God have the right to be themselves, that is to say, the right to be quite concrete personalities with all the positive qualities—as well as limitations—that this supposes. There is much more to these flesh and blood people than simply their founding charism.

Founders and foundresses all had their own temperament and bent. Some were more discursive, while others were more intuitive; some tended to be methodical, while others tended to be spontaneous; some were active and dynamic, while others were taciturn and slow; some were cerebral, while others were emotive. In principle, one would say that none of these features bears directly on the collective vocation of their Institutes. But even here one hesitates to make a hasty or abrupt pronouncement, because the temperament of certain giants of the spirit (Francis of Assisi, Philip Neri, and Ignatius Loyola, for example) seems to have left a deep imprint on the way they lived their religious experiences and on the spiritual doctrine which they left behind. The strength of spirit and deep compassion of Catherine McAuley can still be seen in her daughters, the Sisters of Mercy. Even when certain followers of these founding personalities have different and even opposite temperaments, the fact that the image of their father or mother is proposed to them as an identity model, and the correlative fact that these primal figures helped create an environment in which these "different" disciples must grow tends to act as a corrective and an enriching influence on the latter. There is something of Francesco Bernardone in every Franciscan, something of Inigo de Loyola in every Jesuit, and something of Louise de Marillac in every Daughter of Charity.

Founders and foundresses also had their own opinions, not only in theological matters (and many of them were not Doctors of the Church), but also in philosophical and political matters. So much for such opinions. None of them belongs to their spiritual heritage. Still, there is one special set of opinions that forms a case apart, namely their opinions in matters relating to spiritual theology or to the theology of the religious life. These are more closely connected to the nature of their Institutes.

Certain founders and foundresses were more inclined to some forms of prayer than to others. Being men and women of a certain temperament, living in a determined era and environment, they have had a taste for certain forms of devotional prayer that later fell into disuse. But even in this case we may be dealing with attitudes and preferences that relate to the Institute in the Church and belong to the spiritual heritage of the Institute, while other attitudes may be strictly personal to the founder or foundress. Obviously religious Institutes cannot be permanently conditioned by a bygone era's lack of liturgical sense, when private forms of piety were allowed to flourish like some lush, tropical growth to the detriment of essential forms of worship. On the other hand, a certain emphasis on inwardness or on a certain kind of meditation, especially for those in formation, may very well have an intimate relationship with the mission of the Institute in apostolic communities. In these cases the practice may transcend the merely individual.

An easier question to resolve touches on the mystical gifts or charismatic graces received by founders. A religious experience of this sort is unrepeatable, of course. But the fact that a determined vocation and spirituality have developed in a certain manner in the person from whom a religious community derives has an exemplary value for that community. Even such extraordinary phenomena as the stigmatization of Francis of Assisi, the transverberation of Teresa of Avila, and the great mystic-apostolic experiences of Anthony Mary Claret figure as luminously significant factors in the development of their spiritualities, although they may never be repeated as such in the Servants of God who belong to the religious families founded by these Saints. St. Ignatius Loyola's vision at La Storta contained an explicit message for the whole Society of Jesus. Yet all these *gratiae gratis datae* were of a strictly personal nature. They were granted to these extraordinary men and women in order to facilitate their personal mission in the Church.

More than once in the preceding paragraphs we have touched, even without explicitly using the term, on the human limitations of founders and foundresses. As with every other human being these limitations may come from their own individual bent or from their times and their society. It is a real misfortune that, up to our times, we have been given a sterotyped image and a false hagiography of founders. Out of love for their founders or foundresses, out of a desire to strengthen a sense of belonging among their members (each nation or tribe exalts its heroes in order to bolster a sense of collective identity), or even, in a less worthy vein, out of a sort of collective pride (the glory of the founder is the self-glorification of the Institute) religious families have frequently projected an image of their founders without shadows, all light. There is a resistance to speak of the human limits of our father or mother. Up to a certain point this is understandable insofar as one fears that certain exaggerated discussions of the founder might undermine a sense of belonging in the membership or cast doubt on important aspects of the spiritual heritage of the Institute. Nevertheless, one can carry such defensive attitudes too far, and one must face the fact that it can only be done honestly up to a certain point.

There remains the well-known fact that every notable personage has his or her limits and defects. Sanctity is something that God creates or re-creates on our faults and weaknesses, calling forth our response. The ways of sanctity are also ways of resistance and incomprehension. And grace, even though it exerts a corrective influence on our nature, does not suppress all its limitations. Today, a more balanced and objective attitude in these matters is opening up. Sisters, above all, are now speaking of their foundresses as women in the full sense of the word, who struggled in other times and other societies in search of their own way. Some years ago the author of this study, in an essay on the founder of his own community (an extraordinary Saint in many respects), tried to point out clearly some of the weak spots in his personality.[4] We can only praise the great intellectual honesty and tact with which Brothers Michel Sauvage and Miguel Campos analyzed the concept of obedience and community discipline developed by their founder, St. Jean-Baptiste de La Salle, within his limited historical coordinates.[5] Their example deserves a numerous following.

XII

The Interpretation of the Charism

Perhaps in view of what we have just said the reader may already have come to this conclusion: Every religious Institute, in order to arrive at a clear understanding of its own mission in the Church, must continually return to interpret the charism of its founder or foundress. We stress "to interpret," because, as we have seen, the founder's actuation of the common charism always involves certain factors that proceed from his concrete individuality, situated in a particular time and place. The charism must be continually interpreted because the sons and daughters of founders are subject to the flow of history.

Some religious of a conservative frame of mind are inclined to consider only or mainly what the founder did. By this we do not mean peripheral issues, but central and decisive things the founder did. There are some who dwell on the fact that the founder favored schools or hospitals, without considering that clinics or colleges might have an entirely different meaning. In fact, what the founder did does not necessarily express the vocation of the Institute in a universally valid sense, but rather in the sense that it was the best expression of the vocation in a given set of social circumstances. Indeed, an overly literal or material adherence to the founder's initiatives might limit the growth of the Institute.

On the opposite side, religious of a progressive bent may tend to break with the past and propose a reformulation of the charism in view of the present needs of the Church. Some tend to form an idea of the founding charism that is stripped pretty much to the essentials and is hence expressed in very general terms, and then proceed to use this pared-down idea to justify a number of initiatives, some of which are quite arguable. Here the potential risk to be avoided would be that of the Institute's losing its identity.

This is a very serious matter, not only for the risk it poses for a religious family's fidelity to the inspiration that gave it its being in the Church, but also because charisms are the exclusive property of the Spirit who gives them, not that of the individuals or the group that receives them, and, indeed, not even of the Church for which they are destined. What is required is an attitude of obedience in the New Testament sense, that is to say, an attitude of faith and of humble docility to the Spirit and to the Spirit's action in us. Reflection on the charism of an Institute, just as on the vocation of a person, must begin in prayer and be carried out with a constant contemplative attitude, also in the biblical sense, that is to say, an attitude of listening to the Word of God. The *locus theologicus* for this reflection— this means through which this Word reaches us—is, within the tradition of the Church, the living history of this charism which begins in the founder or foundress and continues in successive generations down to us. Because the charism is already there, given by the Lord to the one who received the original inspiration and lived it in an exemplary way, and given, too, by the same Lord to numerous other disciples of the founder or foundress.

We must then begin with the founder or foundress. Prayerful reflection must commence with a serious historical investigation of the person who gave life to the Institute: a concrete and living person who existed during a determined period of time in the history of the Church, a man or a woman who only gradually came to be aware of his or her own gift and went on interpreting it through successive words and actions which enriched and corrected their earlier interpretations. It is a study, then, of the genesis and development of the charism in this exemplary personality. During this phase we must remain docilely open to the data provided us in the relevant documentation. But we must penetrate these data in an attempt to verify their true meaning. We already remarked that the charism may not be identified *tout court* with what the father or mother did, since their actions were not the charism itself but the way in which they responded to their vocation, within a particular set of historical presuppositions.

As Father Francis, O.M.I., pointed out in his brief but substantial essay[1] the correct attitude in the presence of a founder's charism, is a hermeneutical attitude. In a hermeneutic (interpretative) approach the material facts and initiatives of the founder are looked upon as the point of departure. But these facts are always situated in the social context in which they occurred. Only in this way may they be adequately understood and assessed according to the degree in which they reflect the charism or the time.

This means that what really counts is not so much what founders actually did, but rather what were their intentions, their ideals. In this case, too, it is not the flesh, so much as the spirit, that counts. The past is not *per se* a law for the present but a means through which religious can discover their permanent vocation.

We must go, then, beneath the facts to the deep intentions that motivated them.[2]

But the history of the founding charism does not end with the death of the foundress or founder. This charism has founded the life of the religious family throughout its ensuing times and continues to be the source of its life in the present. The Institute, globally (we must suppose that this is so until the contrary is proved), has been striving to respond to this vocation. And this vocation presents itself with relevant characteristics in the Servants of God who have been sanctified by being faithful to it. Here too, however, our investigation cannot be reduced to a mere collection of facts and data. This is true, in the first place, because in this instance too we are dealing with a series of successive responses to the charism, responses given within determined historical situations. It is true, in the second place, because the past and present history of an Institute can never be canonized. We have to grant the possibility of reductive interpretations and of a greater or lesser deviation from the original inspiration. If Vatican II invites us to return continually to the Gospel and to the original inspiration, it is because infidelity is a distinct possibility. The original inspiration presents itself as a criterion on the basis of which we must judge all successive realizations.

Finally, when we come to reformulate the charism for the present epoch of the Institute, we must also take into account the present situation of the Church and the world. Obviously we do this, not to modify the charism, which does not belong to us, but rather in order to see how we must respond today to these deep intentions of the founder or foundress. Pius XII once told religious Institutes that they must do today what their founders would have done. Certainly they would in some cases do again what they had done then, but it is also clear that some of the initiatives they took in their own day would not be taken by them in our days.

XIII

Charism and Tradition: Living Realities

Before bringing our reflections to a close it might be helpful for us to highlight an idea which was implicit in some of the particular points we discussed: the significance of time as a possibility for growth. In fact, the value of time is not restricted merely to the past, which can only be the object of interpretation. Time also embraces the present and the future, and in these cases time presents itself as a challenge to live.

We have already stated that in every genuine reformulation of a charism—that is, in every reformulation made not merely on the theoretical level of investigation, but on the quite practical level of continuing in history—account must be taken of the present historical situation. Every religious Institute is subject to the ups and downs of history: to periods of progressive enrichment as well as periods of decadence and deviation. This is why the "original inspiration" is so important. In order to change one must have a clear consciousness of one's own identity. Besides, change and creativity are inevitable aspects in the life of every religious family.

To grasp this clearly we must bear in mind that the terms used to express the identity of various Institutes (inspiration, charism, tradition) belong to very dynamic categories of thought. All three pertain to the theology of the Holy Spirit. Whereas *inspiration* refers to the fact of being initially moved and enlightened by the Holy Spirit, a *charism* is a vocational gift granted by the Holy Spirit for the constant building up of the Church, and a *tradition* is the growth and unfolding of the potential of this gift throughout history.

In the Bible, the Spirit is God's self-revelation as giver of life. This life-giving is verified on different levels: the human race in Genesis, the dry bones in Ezekiel, and the Church on Pentecost. The new creation is attributed in a special way to God the Spirit. The special sign of this active presence which renews the face of the earth is prophecy, namely, the charism whereby a human person speaks in the name of God and which frequently presupposes an in-depth knowledge of history.

Every charism, since it is a gift of the life-giving Spirit, is always a dynamic reality, a source of life and activity. The charism given to founders, and after them to their families as a common vocation in the Church, must for that very reason remain the same throughout the length of time and breadth of space. However, because of its pneumatic origin and because of its destination for a Church which moves forward in history, it produces different fruits in different times and places. It gives rise to various styles of life, through which it incarnates the Gospel in different tongues. It impels Institutes to adopt varied forms of ministries. Hence it is essential for religious communities to remain open and docile to the action of the Holy Spirit. Communion with the Spirit is the true source of renewal and adaptation of the religious life.

Two final conclusions seem to impose themselves. First and foremost, the charism is something that must be lived, more than understood, although an understanding of it is an integral part of living it. Individuals and groups must let themselves be animated by it and allow the Spirit of God to shape them by his action. Here again we are brought back to the theme of docility to God's leading. Second, we must face the fact that the charism, properly speaking, cannot be defined. Rather, it must be described by gathering up those traits through which it gradually appeared in those who first lived it, as well as in the successive generations who received it. It is not something that can be expressed in a few words. For if it were reduced to just a few words, many of its really different manifestations in history would seem to blur and coincide.

Notes

NOTES TO FOREWORD

1. AAS *(Acta Apostolicae Sedis)* 16 (1924), 135.

2. LG *(Lumen Gentium),* 45. PC *(Perfectae Caritatis),* 1.2

3. Th. Grzeszczyk, *Il Carisma dei Fondatori* (Roma, 1974), 102 pp.

4. G. Damiza, art. "Fondatore," *Enciclopedia Cattolica,* (Vatican City) I, 1474-1475.

5. Several Authors, art "Fondatore," *Dizionario degli Istituti di Perfezione* (Roma: Ed. Paoline) IV, 96-108.

6. Ch.E. Bouchard, "The Charism of the Community: Does it really make a difference?" RRel 37 (1978), 350-356. N. Brockman, "Directed Prayer and the Founding Charism," RRel 33 (1974), 257-264. Id.—R. Fitz, "The Founding Charism and the Future of Religious Life," *The Ave Mater Dolorosa Supplement* 2 (April 1975), 1-59. Efrén de la Madre de Dios, "Carisma Personal y Carisma Institucional: Contrastes," *Revista Espiritualidad* (1972), 7-25. J. C. Futrell, "Discovering the Founder's Charism," *The Way, Supplement* 14 (Fall 1971), 62-70. F. E. George, "Founding Founderology," RRel 36 (1977), 40-48. J. F. Gilmont, "Paternité et Médiation du Fondateur d'Ordre," RAM 40 (1964), 395-426. F. Juberías, "La Paternidad de los Fundadores," *Vida Religiosa* (1972), 317-328. L. Labonté, "The Founder's Charism and the Primordial Concern of an Institute," in *The Spirit of the Founders and our Religious Renewal,* Vita Evangelica 9 (Ottawa: Canadian Religious Conference, s.a), 393-421. T. Ledochowska, *In Search of the Charism of the Institute* (Rome: Ursulines, s.a.). J. M. Lozano, "Founder and Community: Inspiration and Charism," RRel 37 (1978), 214-236. S. McCarthy, "Touching Each Other at the Roots: A Reflection on the Charism of the Founder," RRel 31 (1972), 202-205.

J. Murphy O'Connor, "The Charism of the Founder," *Supplement to Doctrine and Life* (1974), 10-18. G. Oesterley, "Fundatores Ordinum et Congregationum quinam sint," CpR 27 (1948), 72-75. M. Olphe Galliard, "Le Charism des Fondateurs Religieux," Vie Cons 39 (1967), 338-352. J. M. R. Tillard, *There are Charisms and Charisms* (Bruxelles: Lumen Vitae, 1977).

7. F. Ciardi, *I Fondatori Uomini dello Spirito.* Doct. Diss. Istituto Vita Religiosa, Lateran University, Rome 1981.

8. S. Rituum Congregatio, Sectio Historica, *Inquisitio iussu S.D.N. PII PP XI peracta super dubio: An B. Ludovicus M. Grignion de Monfort historice habe possit uti Fundator, non solum Presbyterorum Missionariorum Societatis Mariae et Fi-liarum Sapientiae, sed etiam Fratrum Instructionis a S. Gabriele* Sect. Hist. n. 47, (Typis Poligl. Vaticanis 1942), 82 pp. The dossier contains, besides historic studies relating to the case, the *vota* or opinions of two consultors of the Congregation of Religious, written in 1909 and 1910. The *votum* of Fr. Placido Lugano, O.S.B., deals with the conditions required in order to acknowledge anyone as a founder. *Nova Inquisitio iussu S.D.N. Pii XII peracta super dubio . . .* (Typis Poligl. Vaticani 1947), 1014 pp. contains, in its Introduction, three brief responses by Fr. Siervo Goyeneche, C.M.F., Cosme Sartori, O.F.M., and Gerard Oesterle, O.S.B. also on the subject of requisites for being termed a founder or foundress. Cf. pp. XV-XVII.

NOTES TO CHAPTER I

1. *Nova Inquisitio,* p. XV.

2. *Nova Inquisitio,* pp. XVI-XVII.

3. *Nova Inquisitio,* p. XV.

4. Cf. A. Ravier, S. J., "Ignace de Loyola fonde la Compagnie de Jésus," *Christus* 36 (1973), 82-99, 230-267.

5. St. Anthony M. Claret, *Constituciones y Textos sobre la Congregación de Misioneros,* ed. J. M. Lozano (Barcelona: Claret, 1971), 338-349.

6. *Normae secundum quas S. Congregatio Episcoporum et Regularium procedere sole in approbandis novis Institutis votorum simplicium,* published by L. R. Ravasi, C. P., *De Regulis et Constitutionibus Religiosorum* (Desclée, 1958), 188-233.

7. Letter of November 25, 1548: *Obras Completas del Santo Maestro Juan de Avila* (B.A.C.; Madrid, 1970) I, p. 118.

8. Notes, by Polanco, ibid. p. 132.

9. R. Tellería, C.SS.R., *San Alfonso de Ligorio* (Madrid 1950), pp. 176-180.

10. Petition to Gregory XVI, with concession appended *ad calcem:* Ms of Caixal in Archives des. Pyrénées Orientales, n. 1925, under Réfugiés espagnols.

11. J. M. Lozano, *Con mi Iglesia te desposaré. Estudio sobre la exper-*

iencia religio sa de la S. de D. M. Antonia París (Madrid, 1974), 146-148.

12. D. Rushe, *Edmund Rice, The Man and His Times,* (Dublin: Gill and Macmillan, 1981), 32.

13. A. Rosmini, *Epistolario Ascético* (Roma, 1912) I, pp. 51-60, 70-74, 91.

14. *Reg. fus.* 8,3; *Reg. brev. Proem.:* PG 31, 940. 1080.

15. RB. Prol. 45.

16. Rule 1223, c. 1.

17. Cf. A. Ravier, "Ignace de Loyola fonde la Compagnie de Jésus," 1.c pp. 82-99.

18. Cf. J. M. Javierre, *Soledad de los Enfermos* (Madrid: B.A.C., 1973).

19. *Inquisitio iussu S.D.N. Pii PP XII,* 1942, p. 74.

20. Art. "Foucauld," *Dizionario degli Istituti di Perfezione* IV, 162-165.

21. L. Verheijen, *La Regle de Saint Augustin,* Paris 1967, 2 vols.

22. Saint Francis of Assisi, *Writings and Early Biographies* (Chicago: Franciscan Herald Press, 1973), 74-76.

NOTES TO CHAPTER II

1. St. Anthony M. Claret, *Escritos Autobiográficos y Espirituales* (Madrid: B.A.C., 1959), 509-510.

2. On the teachings of Pius XII, cf. *Documentos Pontificios sobre la Vida Religiosa,* collected by J. M. Merlín, C.M.F. (Coculsa: Madrid, 1959), 18-20, 32, 42, 104, 118-120, 323. On the teachings of John XXIII, cf. *Juan XXIII y la Vida Religiosa,* collected by C. M. Mesa, C.M.F. (Madrid: Coculsa, 1963), 78-83, 87, 130-131, 245-247. The teachings of Paul VI and John Paul II are referred to in the paragraphs which follow.

3. LG, 45.

4. PC, 2b, *Evangelica Testificatio,* 11.

5. Letter to the First Congress of the States of Perfection, November 12, 1950, *Documentos Pontificios,* p. 36.

6. PC, 2b.

7. *La Vita Religiosa nel Magistero Pontificio Postconciliare,* ed by E. Catazzo O.F.M. (Vicenza, 1969), 27, 103, 216, 305, 330.

8. LG, 45, cited in *Renovationis Causam,* Foreword.

9. *Evangelica Testificatio,* 11.

10. PC, 2b, cited in *Ecclesiae Sanctae* II, 12 and *Evangelica Testificatio,* 11.

11. LG, 45, cited in *Renovationis Causam,* Foreword; P.C. 2b, cited in *Ecclesiae Sanctae* II, 16 and *Evangelica Testificatio,* 11.

12. *Evangelica Testificatio,* 11.

13. *Regiminis Militantis,* 2. *Exposcit Debitum,* 2.

14. Pius VI, Encycl. Letter *Quod Aliquantum,* March 10, 1791.

15. Pius IX, Encycl. Letter, *Ubi Primum,* May 17, 1847.

16. Pius XI, Letter *Unigenitus:* AAS 16 (1924) 135.

NOTES TO CHAPTER III

1. "Ut semper unum primum vocaret," J. Nadal, S. J., "Exhortationes Colonienses 1, 3, in *Commentarii de Instituto Societatis* Iesu (Roma, 1962), 779.

2. 1 Cor. 4:15.

3. PL, 195, 239. Cf. PL, 195, 245.

4. PL, 202, 705.

5. PL, 185, 574.

6. *Les Vies Coptes de Saint Pachôme et de ses premiers successeurs,* ed. by L.Th. Lefort, (Louvain 1943), 55.

7. Flame, II, 12-13.

8. "Exhortationes 1554 in Hispania," nn. 4-5, in *Commentarii,* p. 37.

9. "Exhortationes 1554," n. 6, p. 37.

10. Ibid., n. 7, pp. 37-38.

11. Ibid., n. 6, p. 37.

12. Thomas Aquinas, 3 q 62 a 2.

13. *Autobiographie,* ch. 38, Mss. p. 175; copy p. 135.

14. *Ecrits,* I, p. 770.

15. *Copies de Lettres,* p. 197.

16. *Lettres,* pp. 570, 573; *Autobiographie,* p. 498.

17. *The Way,* 2.5

18. *The Way,* 2,3; 8,2; 13,3; 14,1; 25,1; 26,3.

19. August 31, 1837; December 29, 1837; November 15, 1838; July 27, 1840; September 9, 1840.

NOTES TO CHAPTER IV

1. LG, 42; PC, 12.

2. LG, 43.

3. LG, 43.

4. PC, 1b.

5. PC, 1c.

6. PC, 8.

7. *Evangelica Testificatio,* 11.

8. Disc. "C'est une joie," *L'Osservatore Romano,* March 31—April 1, 1969, p. 1.

9. Disc. "Eccoci felicemente," *L'Osservatore Romano,* September 10, 1971, p. 1.

10. Disc. "Ed ora," *L'Osservatore Romano,* December 30, 1971, p. 2.

11. Letter "Facere et tacere," *L'Osservatore Romano,* March 20-21, 1973, p. 1.

12. Disc. "Hace unos momentos," *L'Osservatore Romano,* January 28-29, 1974, p. 1.

13. To the Superiors General of Men, November 24, 1978, p. 3.

14. To Religious, Sao Paulo, July 3, 1980; July 21, 1980, p. 7.

15. *Origins* 12 (n. 23: November 18, 1982), p. 363, n. 2.

16. *Mutuae Relationes,* I, 3.

17. St. Thomas Aquinas, 1-2 q 111 a 1.

18. 1-2 q 111 a 4.

19. Cf. X. Ducros, art. "Charismes," DSpir, II, 503-507; J. Gewiess—K. Rahner, art. "Charisma," LTK, II, 1025-1030.

20. Note the significant title of T. Pfanner's work *Diatribe de charismatibus sive donis antiquae Ecclesiae,* Gotha 1680.

21. Cf. also Acts 2, 17-21.

22. H. Conzelmann, art. "Charisma," in G. Kittel, *Theol. Dictionary of the New Testament* (Grand Rapids: Eerdmans, 1974), 9, 402-406.

23. 1 Cor. 1:7; cf. 1:4; Rom. 1:11; 5:15 and 16; 6:23.

24. E. Bettencourt, art. "Carismas," in Sacramentum Mundi (Herder: Barcelona, 1972) I, 669-672. A Bittlinger, *Gifts and Ministries,* (Grand Rapids, 1973). Id. *Gifts and Graces* (Grand Rapids, 1976). B. N. Wambecq, "Le mot charisme," NRTh 97 (1975), 345-355.

25. *Sacramentum Mundi,* I, 669-672.

26. St. Thomas Aquinas, 1-2 q 111 a 1.

27. J. M. Lozano, *Discipleship, Towards an Understanding of Religious Life* (Chicago: CCRS 1980), 113-140.

28. L. Labonte, "The Founder's Charism and the Primordial Concern of an Institute," in *The Spirit of the Founders and our Religious Renewal,* Vita Evangelica 9 (Ottawa: Canadian Religious Conference, s.a.), 303.

NOTES TO CHAPTER V

1. St. Athanasius, *Life of Anthony,* 2. in *Early Christian Biographies* (The Fathers of the Church, vol. 15: Washington, D.C., 1952), 135-136.

2. *Les Vies Coptes de saint Pachôme* (Louvain, 1943), 60, 21-65'

3. J. M. Lozano, "La Comunità Pacomiana: dalla comunione all-istituzione" *Claretianum* 15 (1975), 237-267.

4. Palladius, *The Lausiac History,* c. 32.

5. St. Francis of Assisi, *Testament,* in *Writings and Early Biographies* (Chicago: Franciscan Herald Press, 1973), 68.

6. Letter to Bishop Gattinara, in *Words from the Heart, A Selection from the Personal Letters of Saint Paul of the Cross* (Dublin: Gill and Macmillan, 1976), 11-12.

7. J. M. Lozano, *A Mystic and Man of Action, Saint Anthony M. Claret* (Chicago: CCRS, 1977), 103-113.

8. M. Kaupas, The Founding of the Sisters of Saint Casimir (Chicago: CCRS, 1981), 24-25.

9. The locution, absent from Celano's "First Life," appears in his second biography of Francis: "Second Life," I, ch. 6, *Writings and Early Biographies* (Chicago: Franciscan Herald Press, 1972), 370. On Francis' reading the Gospel, cf. "First Life," I, ch 9, ibid., pp. 246-247.

10. P. de Ribadeneyra, S. J. *Vida de Ignacio de Loyola,* I, ch. 7.

11. Ibid., II, ch. 11.

12. *Autobiographie,* ch. 35-39, pp. 160-184.

13. Cf. Letter to bishop Gattinaram, in *Words from the Heart,* pp. 11-14.

14. *Autobiography,* nn. 113-120 (Chicago: CCRS, 1976), 48-50.

15. P. Biver, *Apotre et Mystique, Le Pere Lamy* (Mamers, 1960), 84, 165-166.

16. M. Meda, *Un Romanzo della Grazia, Maria Maddalena dell-Incarnazione,* (Seregno, 1968), 44-45.

17. F. Juberías, C.M.F., *Por su Cuerpo que es la Iglesia* (Madrid, 1973), 11-113.

18. *Autobiographie,* ch. 42, 44, pp. 197-198, 207-208. Cf. J. M. Lozano, *Jeanne Chézard de Matel and the Sisters of the Incarnate Word* (Chicago: CCRS, 1983)

19. E. Zoffoli, *San Paolo della Croce. Storia Critica* (Roma: Generalate C.P., 1963) I, p. 16.

20. T. Grzeszcyk, *Il Carisma dei Fondatori* (Rome, 1974), 21.

21. *Promemorie o Carta di Fondazione di Santa Bartolomea Capitanio,* ed. by her Sisters of Charity, pp. 4-8.

22. E. Nadeau, O.M.I., *Martyre du silence, Mere Marie-Anne* (Montréal, 1957), 48-57.

23. J. Rey, S. J., *Luz de Cristo, P. Benito Menni, O. H. Su Espíritu y Obra* (Madrid, 1967), 209.

24. "Dialogùs II, ch. 1: *Commentarii de Instituto Societatis Iesu,* p. 607.

25. P. Coste, C.M., *The Life and Works of Saint Vincent de Paul,* ch 9 (London: Burns Oates, 1934) I, pp. 144-146.

26. St. Anthony M. Claret, *Constituciones y Textos sobre la Congregación de Misioneros* (Barcelona: Claret, 1972), 11-30.

27. Letter to Bishop Gattinara, in *Words from the Heart,* pp. 11-14.

28. LG, 45.

29. LG, 12.

30. *Catechesis XVI, De Spiritu Sancto,* I, n. 16.

31. *Monumenta Historica S. Dominici,* fasc. II, pp. 190-194.

32. *L'Egoismo Vinto* (Rome, 1869), p. 51. Mss Claret, X, pp. 75 ff.

33. Jerome Nadal, probably taking as his point of departure the contempority of the conversion of Ignatius and the reform of Luther (Exhortationes Colonienses 1567, ch 1: *Commentarii,* pp. 779-780), elaborated a theory, which held that the birth of each Order corresponds to the rise of a heresy (*Annotationes in Constit.* ch 2, nn. 38-39, Ibid., p. 123).

34. 1-2 q 68 a 1 c.

35. Rule 1223, ch. 1. Cf Rule 1221, ch. 1. *Writings and Early Biographies* (Chicago: Franciscan Herald Press, 1973), 57 and 31.

NOTES FOR CHAPTER VI

1. Disc. "Eccoci felicemente," *L'Osservatore Romano,* September 10, 1971, p. 1.

2. St. Bonaventure, *Opera Omnia,* (Quaracchi, 1901), p. 592. On St. Ignatius and doctrine, cf. H. Rahner, Ignatius the Theologian, Engl. tr. (New York, 1968). A. Dulles, "Saint Ignatius and the Jesuit Theological Tradition," *Studies,* XIV/2 (March, 1982). J. W. O'Malley, "The Fourth Vow in its Ignatian Context. A Historical Study," *Studies* XVI/1 (January, 1983). 8-14.

NOTES FOR CHAPTER VII

1. Disc. "Benediciamo il Signore," *L'Osservatore Romano*, March 30-31, 1972, p. 1.

2. *Evangelica Testificatio*, 11.

3. *Introduction a la vie et aux vertus chrétiennes*, c. 2 (Paris, 1954), 12-13.

4. *L'Egoismo vinto* (Rome, 1869), 47.

5. *Flame*, II, 12-13.

6. H. Nadal, "2 Complutens," 35, in *Commentarii*, p. 267.

7. *Autobiography*, n. 1 (Chicago: CCRS, 1976), 2.

8. A. Barrios Moneo, C.M.F., *Mujer Audaz, Santa Micaela del Santísimo Sacramento, su vida, sus empresas, su espíritu* (Madrid, 1968), 331-334. Idem, *Una intervención decisiva en la Vizcondesa de Jorbalán* (Madrid, 1964), 203-209.

9. M. Winowska, *Va' ripara la mia casa. Il vero volto di Angela Truszkowka* (Rome: Paoline, 1974), 223.

10. J. M. Lozano, C.M.F., "La Comunità Pacomiana: dalla comunione all'istituzione," *Claretianum* 15 (1975), 245.

11. *Mutuae Relationes*, I, 3.

NOTES FOR CHAPTER VIII

1. *Discipleship, Towards an Understanding of Religious Life* (Chicago: CCRS, 1980), 24-25.

2. *Discipleship*, pp. 100-103.

3. L.G. 5, in *Documents of Renewal for Religious* (Boston: Saint Paul Editions, 1974), 64.

4. LG 12.

5. *Mutuae Relationes*, I, n. 3.

NOTES FOR CHAPTER IX

1. J. M. Lozano, "La Comunità Pacomiana: dalla comunione all'istituzione," *Claretianum* 15 (1975), 258.

2. C. Esser, O.F.M., *The Origins of the Franciscan Movement*, ch. 3 (Chicago: Franciscan Herald Press, 1970), 137-151.

3. M. de Meulemeester, C.SS.R., *Origines de la Congrégation du Tres-Saint Redempteur*, 2 vols. (Louvain, 1953 and 1957).

4. J. M. Lozano, *Regla y Constituciones de las RR. Misioneras de la Inmaculada Concepción* (Rome, 1967), 47-77.

5. J. de C. Bau, *Biografía crítica de San José de Calasanz* (Madrid, 1949). Cf. L. A. Iranyi, art. "Joseph Calasantius," *New Catholic Encyclopedia* 7, 1115-1117.

6. M. O'Connor, *That Incomparable Woman*, (Montreal, 1962). Cf. M. P. Trauth art. "Ward, Mary," *New Catholic Encyclopedia* 14, 808-809.

7. *Beatif. et Canon. S.D. M. Teresiae a Iesu Gerhardinger* (Rome: SCCS, 1979).

8. M. Brunhilde Probst, *The Burning Seal, Biography of Mother Clara*

Pfaender (Chicago: Franciscan Herald Press, 1960).

9. *Mutuae Relationes,* I, n. 3.

10. P. E. Zoffoli, *San Paolo della*

Croce (Roma: Generalate C.P., 1962) I, pp. 778-802, 817-877, 1103-1112, 1013-1032.

NOTES FOR CHAPTER X

1. Disc. "Eccoci Felicemente," *Osservatore Romano,* September 10, 1971, p. 1.

2. Disc. "Ed Ora," *Osserv. Roman,* December 30, 1971, p. 2.

3. Letter "Facere et Tacere," *Osserv.*

Roman, March 20-21, 1973, p. 1.

4. *Writings and Early Biographies* (Chicago: Franciscan Herald Press, 1973), 68.

5. *Mutuae Relationes,* I, n. 3.

NOTES TO CHAPTER XI

1. A. de Vogüé, O.S.B., *Community and Abbot in the Rule of Saint Benedict,* English transl. (Kalamazoo: Cistercian Publications, 1978), 98-99.

2. Ibid., pp. 5-6.

3. "The Abbot and His Monks," *Cistercian Studies* 6 (1971), 249-254.

4. *Mystic and Man of Action, Saint Anthony M. Claret* (Chicago: CCRS, 1977), 21-35.

5. M. Sauvage—M. Campos, *Saint John Baptist de la Salle. Announcing the Gospel to the Poor,* English tranls. (Romeoville, Ill.: Christian Brothers, 1981), 153-156. The same objective, honest, attitude towards St. Ignatius of Loyola in J. W. O'Malley, "The Fourth Vow in Its Ignatian Context. A Historical Study," in *Studies in the Spirituality of Jesuits* XV/1 (January 1983).

NOTES TO CHAPTER XII

1. "Founding Founderology: Charism and Hermeneutics," RRel 36 (1977), 40-48.

2. J. C. Futrell, "Discovering the Founder's Charism," *The Way, Supplement* 14 (Fall 1971), 67-70.

List of Abbreviations

Documents of Vatican II
  CD = Christus Dominus (Bishops)
  EN = Evangelii Nuntiandi (Missions)
  LG = Lumen Gentium (Church)
  PC = Perfectae Caritatis (Religious Life)

Other Works
  PG = Patrologia Graeca (Migne)
  PL = Patrologia Latina (Migne)
  RB = Rule of St. Benedict

List of Founders, Foundresses, and Communities

Other Names